The National Health [...] [...] profit medical compa[...] smoking clinics aroun[...] [...] qualified doctors, nur[...] [...]ists in its research into nicotine a[...] One of its clients is the NHS.

Robert Brynin is Director of the NHA.

STOP SMOKING FOR GOOD

With the NHA Stop-Smoking Programme

Robert Brynin

CORONET BOOKS
Hodder and Stoughton

First published in Great Britain in 1995 by Hodder & Stoughton
A division of Hodder Headline PLC

A Coronet Paperback

10 9 8 7 6 5 4 3 2 1

British Library Cataloguing in Publication Data

Brynin, Robert
Stop Smoking for Good
I. Title
613.85

ISBN 0 340 63240 2

Typeset by Hewer Text Composition Services, Edinburgh
Printed and bound in Great Britain by Cox and Wyman Ltd, Reading

Hodder and Stoughton
A Division of Hodder Headline PLC
338 Euston Road
London NW1 3BH

Contents

vi

Part Three: Further Help And Information

Foreword

I welcome *Stop Smoking for Good* and am pleased to write this Foreword. There are still about fourteen million cigarette addicts in Britain and we all need to work together to help those who are risking their own health – and that of their families – especially since most smokers today cannot afford their addiction. It is a hard addiction to kick – I know: I smoked for twenty-five years!

I write as President of QUIT, formerly the National Association of Non-Smokers. At QUIT we advise thousands of smokers every year and we know that smokers cannot be bullied into stopping. Many smokers believe they are being targeted as anti-social, but the campaign should not be against smokers, because they are the victims. We should be targeting those who cause the effects of tobacco abuse, not those who suffer. The targets must include the tobacco companies and the government, which permits them to continue to advertise their killer products.

Given that the tobacco industry needs to find three hundred new customers to replace those who die each day, we must find a way of keeping the young away from the drug long enough to avoid the pressure they are under to use it. And let us not be in any doubt that what we are fighting is an addictive drug proven to cause disease and death on a massive scale. In the USA the tobacco industry is fighting desperately for the right to sell innocent people this drug. In the UK, despite a dismal record of official action to curb the activities of the industry, there is a growing momentum, from organizations like ASH, QUIT and now the NHA, towards giving people the right to a smoke-free environment and to protect their children from the pushers.

Since 1990 the NHA, through its research into nicotine addiction, its network of clinics, and its work with employers helping staff to cope with the effects of workplace smoking policies, has been making a growing contribution to the health of the nation. Although lacking funding and support from official sources, it has fought for the right of smokers to be accepted as victims. Alcoholics and hard drug users are given treatment and sympathy, but smoking is still seen as a self-inflicted problem.

The NHA's objective is for the British medical authorities to accept that we have 14 million people who smoke not because they want to, but because they have to. It is time to follow the NHA's example, and treat smokers not as pathetic or weak-willed, but as true drug addicts. Only then will we have a chance of providing real help for them.

The work done by Dr Richard Mackarness on nicotine addiction back in the 1970s will one day be recognized as a major medical breakthrough. The NHA has already understood its value and has worked hard to develop his techniques. We now have a national resource in these clinics which GPs should be urgently investigating.

Meanwhile the NHA has written this invaluable book. Whilst there is no substitute for medical treatment, everyone reading it will benefit – at the very least, from increasing their understanding of their inability to stop smoking. And very many people will, if they follow the three programmes, go on to stop, and stay stopped. The NHA Helpline that can (and should) be used with the programmes is invaluable: no matter how comprehensive a book is, anyone who stops smoking is likely to want answers to their specific problems, or just support from someone who understands and cares.

This book provides the key to the end of your dependence on cigarettes. Forget your previous difficulties; within a few weeks you can join the ever-growing band of non-smokers, and you will feel both fitter and richer.

Rt Hon. Lord Ennals
Former Secretary of State for Health, 1976–9
President of Quit

Part One

Learning How to Stop

1

Before You Get Going

In our clinics we see thousands of smokers who want to stop, and they come to us because they know we have the neutrogen that controls nicotine addiction. The 'magic drops', as they call them, are important. But so is knowledge.

We wrote this book because, before they joined one of our programmes, we felt our patients needed a clear understanding of what stopping smoking really involves. As the book evolved it became apparent that, with the knowledge we could give people, many of them could stop smoking on their own. Not everyone wants to invest in clinical treatment.

This book is for smokers who have tried hard to stop and failed, who desperately want to stop but just can't. If this is you, you should by now be prepared to invest your time and effort in stopping. No longer do you believe in the pills and potions.

Everyone, by definition, can stop smoking. It doesn't matter how many times you have failed – there is a way to succeed. We are not saying you will have stopped smoking by the time you finish this book. What we are saying is that there is a reason for your failure. Time and time again our patients say they just don't know why they failed before

3

they came to us. You will never succeed until you understand why you have failed – otherwise how are you going to
learn from your mistakes?

How to use this book

Don't trust to luck; read the book carefully, understand the
issues, and use the knowledge you gain to deal with them.

There are three distinct stages you will go through when
you stop smoking, whether you do it on your own, with this
programme, or with any other method. Even patients at
NHA Stop-Smoking Clinics go through them. They are:

* **Addiction**: you will have to come off your drug, which is
  no different from coming off any other drug.
* **Convalescence**: we have looked at every known method
  of stopping smoking, and not one of them tackles this
  problem. When you stop smoking, your body reacts
  badly. This is quite separate from addiction. It is likely
  to be a major contributor to your previous failures, so
  you will need to understand it.
* **Psychological dependence**: this includes your fear, your
  belief that you need the drug even after the addiction is
  finished – in fact your dependence in every way other
  than addiction itself.

The book is therefore in two distinct parts:

* Part One, which you have to read to understand how to
  stop smoking.
* Part Two, which is going to lead you through your stop-
  smoking programme.

Part Two itself consists of three programmes for you to
follow:

* **The Preparation Programme** (psychological dependence/
  stress/habit/fear), in which you will use the under-

4

standing gained in Part One to overcome most of the psychological dependence that previously caused you to fail. This is followed by:

* **The Cessation Programme** (addiction/convalescence), in which you stop smoking. Because you will already have dealt with most of the issues that caused you to fail previous attempts, for the first time this will not be as painful as you expect. This is followed by:

* **The Maintenance Programme** (convalescence/psychological dependence), which leads you through the first few weeks as a non-smoker, and makes sure you can face the coming months and years with confidence.

You might think it a bit tedious to go through the Preparation Programme from beginning to end before actually stopping smoking, but this is an extremely powerful technique, so trust us. When we surveyed patients who came to our clinics, and who had previously stopped smoking and restarted, we found that over ninety per cent only restarted when they came under stress. The inescapable conclusion is that, if you want to stay stopped, you have to deal with stress, even if you feel it has nothing to do with your smoking.

If you are not sure about anything, call our Helpline, which is available to you at any time for as long as you need. Because we are a national non-profit research organization we welcome a chance to talk to you – we can learn as much from you as you can from us. The Helpline is open Monday to Friday from 9am to 6pm.

You've heard it all before – haven't you?

You can rest assured that we would not have written this book unless we had something new and important to say. Here are some curious facts which you might not know:

* When you stop smoking, the way your body regulates your blood sugar will change. Smokers often mistake the symptoms of hypoglycaemia (low blood sugar level) for withdrawal symptoms, and then compound the problem by eating more sugar.
* The main way in which smoking helps you cope with stress is by relieving low-level craving. In other words, it actually sets you up for stress and then relieves it, so you learn to believe that it helps.
* Although you might have been told that psychological dependence is your biggest problem, you would never have had time to become dependent if you had not become addicted to nicotine first – probably within days of starting to smoke.
* Vegetables such as tomatoes, potatoes, aubergines and peppers can make you smoke again, because they are in the same plant family as tobacco. This does not mean you have to stop eating them – just be aware of the issue in case it causes a problem.

This is a serious book, because stopping smoking is a serious subject. But that does not mean it is difficult to follow; on the contrary, it has been designed to be an enjoyable read and a valuable experience. Other people write books that are supposed to be a quick fix; at the NHA we do not have quick fixes. If you have been through that experience before, you should now be ready to take our advice, learn from our experience and succeed.

This book contains a lot of truths that we have had to learn the hard way from our patients. Before you start, we would like you to consider something you might never have realized:

* You currently have a problem – you smoke but you don't want to. You think the problem lies in wanting to stop, but it doesn't – it exists because you started. All of

this problem has been created by tobacco. Therefore your current problem will last only as long as it takes to stop smoking. The problem will go away.

2

Why Don't All Smokers Want to Stop?

MOST OF THEM DO, BUT THEY DON'T
BELIEVE THEY CAN. IF YOU DON'T BELIEVE
YOU CAN, YOU MUST BE WRONG.

Some of the questions answered in this chapter:

* If smoking is as dangerous as we're told, why are 14
  million people still doing it?
* What is the point of stopping if I'm over sixty?
* How can I be expected to stop while society and the
  government condone smoking?

If smoking is really dangerous, why would anyone still do
it? The obvious answers you would get if you asked people
in the street would be:

* Because I enjoy it.
* Because I can't stop.
* Because I need it when I'm stressed.
* Because I've never thought seriously about stopping.
* Because all my friends do.
* Because I'm too young for it to matter.
* Because I'm too old for it to matter.
* Because I've got to die somehow, so why not enjoy it?

You might well have said one of these, or something similar,
in the past. All of them are, of course, nonsense.

The reason people still smoke, and don't want to give up,
is very important to you right now. It will help you

understand why you have had such difficulty in the past, even though you actually want to stop.

There is a simple answer and a complicated answer. The simple answer is that 14 million people in Britain smoke – and how could 14 million people be doing something utterly stupid, that is making them poorer, is affecting their every-day health and is going to shorten their lives? After all, most of them are, presumably, law-abiding people with some intelligence. So, despite all the fuss made to the contrary, it must be all right. That's what a lot of smokers think, anyway.

Now for the complicated answer. If by some miracle the government instituted a real campaign to get people off tobacco, and 7 million people actually did it over the next year (this is entirely possible – not the bit about the government, which would be unthinkable, but the bit about 7 million smokers stopping), you would probably be one of the 7 million. And if you were not, you would probably be so impressed that you would be in the second 7 million. Put simply, people smoke because other people do. And those smokers who don't want to stop often don't want to because other smokers don't want to.

It's a bit like being on a sinking ship. The ship always felt safe before, and now, just because it's listing a little, the crew want you to jump over the side. Perhaps the ship will right itself. Perhaps another ship will come to the rescue. Failing these, you are going to have to abandon ship – to jump into the unknown without knowing how long it will take to be rescued, or whether you will ever be rescued at all.

The 14 million people who still smoke are sailing on the SS *Smoking*. So what if the ship is listing rather badly now? It's still afloat, and 14 million people are clinging to it with you. Some are jumping but you can't see them – they might not have survived. So long as smokers cling to the ship, the nightmare of jumping might go away.

10

Unfortunately, this is one problem you cannot walk away from. Every day you smoke you are in deeper water.

'Because I enjoy it'

On one special day each March hundreds of thousands of smokers can be seen jumping over the side with their eyes shut because they heard the order to abandon ship — otherwise known as National No Smoking Day. But if these people don't want to stop on 364 days of the year, why do they suddenly answer the call on the 365th?

The fact is, they *do* want to stop. And here we have one of the many contradictions encountered in stopping smoking. Why does someone who, deep down, wants to stop, persist with the excuse: 'Because I enjoy it'? If we could answer this question, we could start to solve the riddle of the nation's smoking problem.

In fact we can.

Let's look at the excuses/reasons for not wanting to stop that were listed on p. 9. They won't all apply to you, but they will all give you food for thought. And let's start with that idea of enjoyment.

We won't try to convince you that you don't enjoy smoking, even though it is not the enjoyment you think it is (Chapter 8 explains why). Let's look at it another way, and ask: is enjoyment a reason for continuing to smoke? How much do you enjoy smoking? And do you enjoy all the cigarettes you smoke?

Exercise
Calculate the financial cost of smoking each year. Assuming you smoke twenty a day, that represents about £800 a year of your (taxed) income. Consider what else you could get for £800, like a second holiday every year. Is the enjoyment of smoking better than that of two holidays a year?

11

This is not a trick question, because in reality many smokers would say, 'No, I would rather smoke – much as I would like two holidays a year.' The interesting point is *why* you make this choice, which we shall come to a little later.

'Because I can't stop'

Why can't you stop? If you knew the answer to that, you would have done it long ago. But for the purpose of this argument let's dispute the fact.

You say you don't want to stop because you can't. This makes some sense – but not a lot. Perhaps what it means is that, since you couldn't stop anyway, there is no point in wanting to, just as there is no point in wanting anything you cannot have – an idea we retain from childhood.

Exercise

You have to understand why you don't want to stop. If you could overcome the problem – in other words, if you could find a guaranteed way to stop smoking – would you definitely want to? Most mature smokers would almost certainly want to stop if it were guaranteed with any particular method. So if you can say for sure that you would want to stop if it were guaranteed, then all you have to do is find that method and your motivation will soar. Then, bingo! You will be a non-smoker. So far, so good.

'Because I need it when I'm stressed'

If smoking helps with stress – and that's a big 'if' – wouldn't it be better to go on smoking? If you need to smoke to deal with the stresses in your life, isn't this a valid reason for continuing?

The fact is that there are very few people for whom

smoking is, on balance, better than stress. There are two issues here. First, why is it that both non-smokers and ex-smokers survive quite well without cigarettes? It's because when you smoke, you *believe* you need to do so in order to handle stress. Any addict would. Second, is the harm that smoking does an acceptable price to pay to deal with stress?

Exercise

Ask yourself whether the price you pay to smoke is worth it. For example, if you are worried about money, and you smoke twenty a day, how is spending £800 a year going to help? If you are worried about your health, how is doing something guaranteed to make it worse going to help? If you are worried about someone else's health, how is being £800 a year poorer and less healthy going to help? Just how does smoking help with any of the specific problems you have to deal with?

There are in fact two ways in which it helps. First, it is a narcotic drug, so it dulls the brain, and thus appears to remove the problem. But it doesn't actually remove the problem, and you know it doesn't. Second, as long as you believe it helps, then it does. Addicts always believe their drug helps. As long as you believe it helps, that is a good reason for not wanting to stop. Once you have reasoned that you would actually be better off without cigarettes, you will have a reason for stopping.

'Because I've never thought seriously about stopping'

Most mature smokers have thought about stopping. Younger smokers tend to live in a make-believe world where old age, infirmity and death are a long way off. When you reach the age of thirty they are a little closer, and by forty you start to see them rather more clearly. By fifty these events have already happened to some of your friends and family; and you know that, come hell or high water, they are going to happen to you.

Maybe the reason you now want to stop is no more than that. Or maybe you did think about it before, but not seriously for any of the reasons we are discussing here. For example, you might not have believed you would be able to stop, so the idea remained a vague desire and never developed into a definite want.

Exercise
If you haven't thought seriously about stopping before, why do you want to now? In fact, *do* you want to stop? Try writing down your reasons. Health might come first, particularly if you are getting on in years or if you have recently developed some smoking-related illness.

Now ask yourself the question again, but in a different way. If you have a particular reason for stopping now, why didn't that reason exist before?

Health: as we have just seen, age has a great deal to do with the matter.

Money: this is a little strange for many people, because age tends to bring greater financial resources. Teenagers want to smoke but cannot afford to; retired people can often afford to but want to stop. So is money really an issue for you? It might be if you are a single parent, say, or unemployed. This does not necessarily mean, however, that you want to stop smoking; it might only mean that you cannot afford to smoke, which is not the same thing. Whilst it might be important to you, we know from experience that financial hardship is a poor motivator where giving up smoking is concerned.

Social pressure: this is the real reason. Teenagers are under pressure to smoke from their peers. As smokers get older, this pressure decreases and the pressure to stop increases. Although almost all smokers quote health as their main reason for wanting to stop, they underestimate the effect of social pressure from friends, family, the media and the medical profession. So, as you get older, you move from having no good reason to stop, to having just that. Of course, the reasons were there all the time – it just took time to see them. That is one of the terrible tragedies of smoking.

'Because all my friends do'

As we have just seen, peer pressure is the main reason why young people start to smoke. It also keeps them at it even if they find they hate it. After a very short while peer pressure is no longer needed, because addiction and then psychological dependence take over.

The reason your friends smoke might be that their friends do. And the reason their friends do is that *their* friends do. And they smoke because you do.

This is not a reason, it is an excuse. The reason is addiction and psychological dependence. Face that fact now.

Exercise

Imagine this scenario. All your smoking friends are gathered in one room; a magician enters, waves his magic wand, and they all stop smoking there and then and never think about cigarettes again. Would you want to be in the room with them? If the answer is yes – and it almost certainly will be – the reason you smoke is not because all your friends do. You all smoke because you cannot stop. If the answer is no, either you are deceiving yourself or you really don't want to stop smoking. (In which case, why are you reading this book?)

'Because I'm too young for it to matter'

In some ways, smokers under thirty are right: the incidence
of smoking-related disease below that age is low. And that's
precisely how the tobacco companies stay in business.
Smoking shortens your life, but most people feel little or
no ill effect in their first thirty years of smoking. If there
were high emphysema or lung cancer rates among smokers
in their twenties, the tobacco companies would have gone
bust long ago.

So, in a way, in your twenties you are too young for it to
matter. For two reasons, though, that viewpoint is terribly
and tragically wrong. First, all the time you are smoking
you are developing smoking-related disease. It might take
thirty years to matter, but as long as you are smoking that
time is coming. Second, you might think you can smoke for
thirty years before it matters, but by then you are likely to
be hopelessly addicted and dependent, so you will not be
able to stop even if you want to. It will be too late.

Exercise
Ask yourself whether you still feel you can get away with
smoking because of your age. If you think you can, you are
looking for an excuse. As you have just read, the excuse is a
futile one. You are only getting into deeper water.

'Because I'm too old for it to matter'

The ages of patients in our clinics range from thirty (see
p. 193), the youngest we will accept, to over eighty. The
older ones sometimes ask us if there is any point in stopping
at their age. What they mean is, will there be any benefit; or
to put it more strongly, will the benefit outweigh the
disadvantages – by which they mean the effort.

Given that it takes some years to recover fully from the

damage done by smoking, and that recovery is slower in older people, it might not be worth their while stopping. There are, in fact, two disadvantages to consider.

The first is the effort involved in stopping. If stopping is painful, perhaps it shouldn't be attempted. Interestingly, patients who have smoked for over half a century seem to have no more difficulty stopping than anyone else. In fact, we often note a certain quiet resolve in them which is lacking in younger people. Perhaps it is because they know they have nothing to lose.

And in any case, why *should* stopping be painful? An eighty-year-old is not necessarily going to be any more addicted than a twenty-year-old, and it is breaking the addiction (if it is done without medical help) that hurts. The difference is the habit; it is not quite so easy to change a sixty-year habit as a ten-year one.

The second disadvantage is the loss of the 'enjoyment' of smoking. We shall be looking closely at this idea of 'enjoyment' later, but for now we have to concede that, if a smoker believes in the 'enjoyment', sixty years are going to reinforce that belief more than ten years are.

Now we need to weigh against these two disadvantages the reasons why stopping smoking is so important in old age. As you get older, your body's ability to heal itself deteriorates. When you were younger, you had the strength to fight the damage that smoking was inflicting on you, but in old age you have less and less chance of winning. In addition, each cigarette you smoke is harming you, but conversely each day you don't smoke you are not harming yourself. And consider whether, as you get older and more infirm, you really want to abuse your body. A fit and healthy old age is infinitely better than one in which you need constant medical attention.

17

Exercise

Ask yourself whether you would prefer to face old age with a smoking-related disease or without it. You might already have such a condition, but the question is still important. Do you want to do the best for your body or not?

'Because I've got to die somehow, so why not enjoy it?'

This is the ultimate drug addict's nonsense. If it doesn't matter how you die, or even when, why do you look before crossing the road? Getting killed by a 38-tonne truck is usually easier than a slow, agonizing death from lung cancer.

By the time you are in your thirties or forties, you have grown out of this sort of stuff. If only we could teach our children what rubbish it is.

Exercise

Ask yourself how seriously you take the issues, particularly health. The only really valid reason for stopping smoking is that it shortens your life. (It might be, of course, that living is not of interest to you – in which case, be aware that smoking is one of the slowest, most expensive and most anti-social ways to commit suicide.) Do you genuinely believe that smoking will shorten your life, and will also damage your health during that life? If you do, stop deceiving yourself that you don't care. If you don't, stop deceiving yourself that you want to stop smoking.

The real reasons

There are three main reasons why people don't want to stop smoking.

* They are addicted to nicotine. It is unreasonable to expect addicts to *want* to give up their drug.

18

* Because they are addicted, they don't believe they *can* stop. This belief is confirmed for them by the medical profession, which largely has no idea how to help them, and blames them for their problem.
* Society not only condones tobacco products, but actively participates in their manufacture and sale.

There is, of course, no easy answer. At the NHA we are concerned not just with individual smokers, but with social attitudes to smoking and with government involvement in the trade. You, understandably, are concerned with your own problem.

The social factor

In the next generation or two we are unlikely to see any significant shift away from social acceptance of the tobacco industry. You are simply going to have to accept that you want to stop using a lethal drug that is on sale in every supermarket and corner shop; that, as hard as you have tried to come off the drug, the government takes a large cut of the trade's proceeds but then gives its GPs and NHS the power to decide to refuse treating patients who are suffering the consequences of tobacco abuse.

All around you people are buying and smoking the drug, but you have to convince yourself that your decision to come off it is right. The only help we can offer at this stage is to ask you to remember two things:

* The government has no interest in helping. If it did, why would it permit the sale of a drug that kills three hundred times as many people as AIDS?
* Other smokers continue to use the drug, not because they want to, but because they are addicted. They, like you, are victims. You, unlike them, are doing something about it.

The hopelessness factor

As we have seen, many people don't want even to attempt to stop smoking, simply because they are afraid of failure. This applies to men and women in different ways. Men are better able to stop than women are (see below), but often find it harder to take the loss of face that goes with failure. So they cover their fear with bravado – they say they don't want to stop. If this applies to you, now is the time to come to terms with it. Forget your pride – years of your life are too high a price to pay for pride.

Women tend to be afraid of failure for a more important reason. They find it harder to stop than men, and often tell us in our clinics that it is because they have to endure more stress. But this is not the real reason. First, women are likely to become more addicted, on average, than men; this is because women's bodies adapt differently from those of men to the poison that nicotine undoubtedly is. And second, partly because of this stronger addiction they have a greater psychological dependence.

Currently more men than women are stopping smoking – although, interestingly, women far outnumber men in NHA clinics (this probably reflects men's resistance to accepting medical help more than anything else). If you are a woman who is afraid of trying to stop smoking, read right through this book before making a decision: it will make the whole thing look more attainable and less frightening.

The addiction factor

If tobacco wasn't addictive, it is probable that only a few people would start to smoke. And those who did would get fed up trying to adapt to it. It is the addiction that keeps the tobacco industry afloat. It is the addiction that capture smokers, then makes them psychologically dependent.

Until recently, the medical profession has had no idea how to treat nicotine addiction. Doctors have toyed with tobacco substitutes but they are not a cure – which you might have discovered for yourself. For this reason, you might have come to believe that you will never overcome the addiction. Please think about two things:

* If you haven't smoked for about a week, you are no longer addicted to nicotine. You may think you are, which is psychological dependence, but in fact you are not. If you can get through this one week, you have beaten the addiction. But don't do it this way. Follow the Preparation Programme properly, and leave the addiction to last. You might be surprised at how much of your fear of the addiction will have gone by then, because you will be more in control.
* If you really cannot handle the withdrawal symptoms, medical help is now available. Ask your GP in the first place. If he or she doesn't offer Addiction Neutralization Therapy (A.N.T.), ask the doctor to contact us at the NHA for information. We will help the surgery to set up a programme for its patients.

We have now answered these questions:

* If smoking is as dangerous as we're told, why are 14 million people in the UK still doing it?
  Because they have no choice. These 14 million people are addicted to nicotine. No matter how dangerous smoking is, the addiction is not going to go away. Until the authorities change their policy, the 300 smokers who die each day will be replaced by 300 new teenage smokers to benefit the tobacco industry and the Treasury.
* Is there any point in stopping if I'm over sixty?
  There certainly is. Smoking makes you unhealthy;

when you are young poor health can be overcome, but not when you are old.
* How can I be expected to stop while society and the government condone smoking?

The only sensible answer is that you have to accept responsibility yourself. If you wait for the government to ban a drug that kills 111,000 people a year you will be long dead.

3

Why Can't *You* Stop Smoking?

IF YOU KNEW THAT, IT WOULD BE
DIFFERENT NEXT TIME, WOULDN'T IT?
WHEN YOU UNDERSTAND, YOU CAN
SUCCEED.

Some of the questions answered in this chapter:

* Am I addicted to smoking?
* Does habit stop me giving up?
* Am I using smoking to help with stress?

If you knew why you can't stop smoking, you would
presumably be able to do something about it. This seems
logical; but it isn't that simple. It's rather like saying 'If we
knew what was wrong with the nation's economy we could
fix it', or even 'If we knew how to cure cancer we would do
so.' We know how to make car engines that are twice as
economical as the present type, but we don't make them.
We know how to cure Crohn's disease (one of the two
inflammatory bowel disorders), but we don't use the cure.
The reasons why we don't always do what we are able to are
usually political and economic, because these considera-
tions outweigh the benefits.

   You could stop smoking now, but you don't because the
difficulties outweigh what you consider to be the benefits of
smoking. People who come to NHA Stop-Smoking Clinics
pay us because the cost of treatment is less than the
difficulty they would experience without our help. What

they haven't done is analyse why they can't stop smoking and what they need to do about it. Given the dearth of worthwhile information and support, let alone actual medical treatment for what is, after all, a serious medical problem, they cannot be blamed.

Over a number of years we have treated thousands of smokers in NHA clinics, and we have learnt a lot. So let's start uncovering why *you* can't stop smoking. Here is the truth:

YOU ARE ADDICTED TO NICOTINE
YOU USE CIGARETTES TO DEAL WITH STRESS
YOU ENJOY SMOKING
YOU GIVE IN TO THE HABIT

There are no other reasons, even though you may believe there are others. What you are going to do now is learn to fit your perceived reasons into these four, because they inevitably do fit. All four reasons are dealt with in detail in later chapters, but for now let's just look at the basics.

You are not addicted to smoking: smoking is not an addiction. Nicotine is an addictive drug, and smoking is merely the delivery method. Smokers who use nicotine patches prove this – as long as they have a patch on, they can usually survive without a cigarette.

Exercise 1

So now ask yourself the real question: am I addicted to nicotine? Most smokers say they are, but frankly they don't really know. In fact most of them are, even though they don't know how to tell. The mere fact that you keep smoking doesn't prove you are addicted. The only way to find out is to stop. If you suffer withdrawal symptoms you are addicted. If you don't, you might still be addicted partly because some people take a long time to withdraw, and partly because not all smokers can distinguish genuine withdrawal symptoms from ordinary bad temper. Typical symptoms could be involuntary shaking, headaches, a tight chest and sweating. Hypoglycaemia may also be a problem here (see p. 6).

However, it is safe to say that if you suffer withdrawal symptoms within hours of waking up and not smoking, you are addicted.

This is the first reason you can't stop smoking. See Chapters 5 and 6 for more information on addiction.

Exercise 2

Have you ever stopped smoking and then started again? Why did this happen? For most people, stress is the cause.

Do you find yourself smoking more heavily in a stress situation? Do you find yourself desperate to smoke when you have had a shock? Do you notice a marked calming effect when you take the first drag?

If you answer yes to any of these questions, you clearly use smoking to deal with stress.

This is the second reason you can't stop smoking. See Chapter 9 for more information on stress.

Exercise 3

Ask yourself if you enjoy smoking. Ignore the enjoyment of the first cigarette in the morning, because that is addiction. Are there times of the day, for instance when you are socializing, when you particularly enjoy a cigarette? Have you ever thought that you would really like to stop smoking if only you didn't enjoy it so much?

Enjoyment is not difficult to explain, but it is the most insidious reason why people can't stop smoking. This is because there are two types of enjoyment – physical and mental. The physical enjoyment is real, because you are using a narcotic drug. The mental enjoyment is just what it says – it is all in the mind.

This is the third reason you can't stop smoking. See Chapter 8 for more information on enjoyment.

Exercise 4

As you will be reading later, habit is never a reason why people can't stop smoking – it is always, without exception, an excuse. You are certainly in the habit of smoking, but that is not the same as being unable to stop *because* of the habit.

Ask yourself if you have ever said, to yourself or to anyone else, that you cannot stop because of the habit. Most smokers would have to admit to this. If you have, it is not the habit that is the reason, but your belief in the habit. In other words, you give in to the habit.

This is the fourth reason you can't stop smoking. See Chapter 5 for more information on habit.

Exercise 5

Ask yourself if there are any other reasons. As you think of each one, see if it fits into one of the four categories above. You will find that it does.

For example, you might say you fail when you go out with friends, because you need to smoke in company. This is habit: if you didn't go out with your friends for a month, the problem would disappear. Or you might say you *could* change this habit of smoking with your friends, but that you feel more comfortable with a cigarette in your hand and would not enjoy their company as much without. No matter how long you stopped socializing, you might say, you feel you would need a cigarette in your hand when you started again. In this case you feel stressed when you are in company, and you need a cigarette to overcome this stress. In neither case is your social life the real reason – it is only the *perceived* reason.

We are going to look at every single issue you have to face when you stop smoking. We are going to make sure they all fit into our four categories, and then we are going to look at how you can overcome these four problems.

And there is not going to be anything else. If you think there is, go back over this chapter again and make sure you understand it fully before you read on.

This doesn't mean, however, that these four problems are going to be easy to overcome. What we *are* saying is that there are reasons for everything in life, including not being able to stop smoking. There is nothing mysterious about these reasons, but because the problem is caused by a complex mix of issues, each feeding off the others, they can seem too confusing to overcome. If we separate them out they will become manageable.

We have now answered these questions:

* Am I addicted to smoking?
    No. No one is addicted to smoking. But you are probably addicted to nicotine. You can prove this by using nicotine patches – it is the drug, not the cigarette, which satisfies your craving. This proves that addiction to the drug is actually the most important element in stopping smoking. If you smoke twenty a day, you are getting over seventy thousand shots of nicotine each year. If you smoke forty a day, in the last twenty years you will have administered to yourself 3 million shots of nicotine, a drug every bit as addictive as heroin. Never again believe that addiction is all in the mind.

27

* Does habit stop me giving up?

   No. As long as you are addicted you will remain psychologically dependent, and as long as you are dependent you will use habit as an excuse. It can be clearly demonstrated that habit cannot make anyone smoke, but don't confuse habit with addiction.

* Am I using smoking to help with stress?

   You may think you are but, because smoking actually causes stress as well, you are gaining nothing. But as long as you are a smoker, and long afterwards (the length of time varies from smoker to smoker), you will believe in smoking to help with stress.

4

You Do Want to Stop Smoking – Don't You?

YOUR MOTIVATION QUESTIONNAIRE

The more you want to stop smoking, the easier it is going to be. This sounds obvious, and yet most people who try to stop are not truly honest about their motivation. Every year, tens of thousands of people try – and fail. They would all say that they want to stop but don't manage it.

And yet, everyone who wants to stop smoking can do so. To say that it is impossible for some people to stop is nonsense. Is there anything else in your life which you would find impossible to stop doing? Now be honest. Giving up cigarettes is difficult, but not impossible. You might think you're a special case, but you aren't. That's just an excuse in case you fail.

So, on the understanding that somewhere out there is the means for you to become a non-smoker, what we have to figure out is not whether this can be achieved, but how. We are no longer saying 'if' – the words are 'how' and 'when'.

You think this is hype to get you in a positive frame of mind? Not true. Being positive is certainly very helpful in anything you tackle, but you might be surprised at the number of people who fail to stop smoking because they don't face facts. To stop smoking you are going to need to be in control, and control comes with knowledge, which leads to decisions – real decisions, not wishful thinking.

How many people have you heard say, 'I gave up smoking easily. I just decided to do it and did it. I can't understand what all the fuss is about'? An awful lot of these people are kidding themselves. They have forgotten the withdrawal symptoms. And if it was that easy, why do so many of them still get cravings after five or even ten years? And if they still get cravings after ten years, what was it like after two days?

Now why would we make such a strong point about the difficulties you are going to face? Because time and time again we see people who try to stop, find themselves faced with some difficulty, and cave in. The difficulty surprises them, and it overcomes their motivation like a tidal wave.

We have already established that the means are there for you to stop smoking. What we now need to discover is whether you have enough motivation. Motivation does not mean that you want to do something; as noted earlier, it is very easy to want something which you have little chance of getting. First ask yourself how you express that want. Do you say to people, 'I should like to give up smoking', or do you say, 'I want to give up'? Thinking that something would be nice is not the same as wanting it. It would be nice to be a millionaire, but people who become millionaires generally set out with a serious want to do so; the rest of us would rather like to become millionaires but our want is not serious enough.

The key to wanting something seriously is to know *why* you want it. 'Because it would be nice' never made anyone a millionaire, and it will not stop you smoking. So we are going to look, not at how much you want stop smoking, but at *why* you want to. Only when you have understood your reasons will you know whether they are good enough to carry you through to the achievement of your goal.

Questionnaire

Tick in the space provided unless requested otherwise:

Q1

Why do you want to stop smoking? Place these reasons in descending order of importance to you, from 1 to 5

    A Health . . .   B Money . . .   C Social . . .
    D Work policy . . .   E Hate being dependent . . .

Q2

Do you suffer any ill health, definitely or probably caused by smoking (include lack of breath, frequent infections etc.)?

    A Yes . . .   B No . . .

Q3

If you stopped smoking, how much would you hope that your health and fitness would improve?

    A Not at all . . .   B Slightly . . .   C Quite a lot . . .
    D A lot . . .   E Completely . . .

Q4

Do you know anyone who suffers from a serious tobacco-related illness?

    A Yes . . .   B No . . .

Q5

Have you ever known anyone who died from a tobacco-related illness?

    A Yes . . .   B No . . .

Q6

Have you ever known anyone who smoked heavily but still lived to a healthy old age?

    A Yes . . .   B No . . .

Q7

How much chance do you think there is of smoking affecting the health of your lungs?

A None . . .   B Slight . . .   C Quite a lot . . .
D A lot . . .   E Extreme . . .

Q8

What about your heart?

A None . . .   B Slight . . .   C Quite a lot . . .
D A lot . . .   E Extreme . . .

Q9

If it were proved that smoking definitely did not damage health, would you still be so interested in stopping?

A Yes . . .   B No . . .

Q10

In that case, would you be likely to increase your smoking?

A Yes . . .   B No . . .

Q11

Can you comfortably afford to smoke at your present level?

A Yes . . .   B No . . .

Q12

At what point would you be forced to try to stop smoking? When the cost increased by:

A 25 per cent . . .   B 50 per cent . . .
C 75 per cent . . .   D 100 per cent . . .
E 150 per cent . . .   F 200 per cent . . .

Q13

If the cost of smoking were halved (say by reducing the tax), would you still be so interested in stopping?

A Yes . . .   B No . . .

Q14
In that case, would you be likely to increase your smoking?
    A Yes . . .   B No . . .

Q15
Do you feel under pressure (from family/friends/the media) because you are a smoker?
    A Yes . . .   B No . . .

Q16
If you do, do you resent it?
    A Yes . . .   B No . . .

Q17
Do you think non-smokers have a right to a smoke-free environment (say at work, on public transport, in restaurants)?
    A Yes . . .   B No . . .

Q18
Do you think smokers have a right to smoke in public places?
    A Yes . . .   B No . . .

Q19
What proportion of your family and friends smoke?
    A Less than a quarter . . .   B A quarter . . .
    C Half . . .   D Three-quarters . . .
    E Over three-quarters . . .

Q20
If it were completely socially acceptable to smoke, would you still be so interested in stopping?
    A Yes . . .   B No . . .

Q21

In that case, would you be likely to increase your smoking?
  A Yes . . .   B No . . .

Q22

Have you ever felt determined to carry on smoking BECAUSE of the pressure to stop?
  A Yes . . .   B No . . .

Q23

Do you welcome the social pressure against smoking as the push you need to try to stop, and therefore a good thing?
  A Yes . . .   B No . . .

Q24

Who do you blame most for your difficulty in stopping?
  A The tobacco industry, the government, doctors . . .
  B Yourself . . .

Q25

Place the following obstacles to stopping smoking in descending order of importance for you, from 1 to 3
  A Habit . . .   B Addiction . . .   C Enjoyment . . .

Q26

Have you tried to stop smoking before?
                          A No . . .
  Successfully for   B days . . .
                     C weeks . . .
                     D months . . .
                     E years . . .
(tick more than one if you stopped on more than one occasion)

Q27

Have you tried unsuccessfully to stop?
A once . . .   B twice . . .   C more . . .

Your score

First mark your questionnaire according to the answers below. There are no right or wrong answers; the questionnaire has been carefully designed to assess your motivational profile against an ideal.

Q1

If A = 1 score 3	If B = 1 score 0	If C = 1 score 0		
2 score 4	2 score 3	2 score 1		
3 score 2	3 score 4	3 score 2		
4 score 1	4 score 2	4 score 4		
5 score 0	5 score 1	5 score 3		
If D = 1 score 0	If E = 1 score 4			
2 score 1	2 score 3			
3 score 2	3 score 2			
4 score 3	4 score 1			
5 score 4	5 score 0			

Q2
Yes = 2   No = 0

Q3
A = 0   B = 1   C = 2   D = 3   E = 4

Q4
Yes = 1   No = 0

Q5
Yes = 1   No = 0

Q6
Yes = 0   No = 1

Q7
A = 0   B = 1   C = 2   D = 3   E = 4

Q8
A = 0   B = 1   C = 2   D = 3   E = 4

Q9
Yes = 3   No = 0

Q10
Yes = 0   No = 3

Q11
Yes = 0   No = 2

Q12
A = 5   B = 4   C = 3   D = 2   E = 1   F = 0

Q13
Yes = 3   No = 0

Q14
Yes = 0   No = 3

Q15
Yes = 0   No = 1

Q16
Yes = 0   No = 2

Q17
Yes = 1   No = 0

Q18
Yes = 1   No = 0

Q19
A = 4   B = 3   C = 2   D = 1   E = 0

Q20
Yes = 3   No = 0

Q21
Yes = 0   No = 3

Q22
Yes = 0   No = 1

Q23
Yes = 2   No = 0

Q24
A = 1   B = 0

Q25
If A = 1 score 0	If B = 1 score 2	If C = 1 score 0
2 score 2	2 score 1	2 score 1
3 score 0	3 score 0	3 score 2

Q26
A = 0   B = 1   C = 2   D = 4   E = 6

Q27
A = 4   B = 2   C = 0

Q28
Yes = 1   No = 0

Q29
Yes = 0   No = 1

Q30
Yes = 0   No = 2

Q31
Yes = 0   No = 2

Q32
Yes = 0   No = 1

Q33
Yes = 0   No = 1

Q34
Yes = 0   No = 1

Q35
Yes = 2   No = 0

What your score means

The maximum you can score is ninety-five, the minimum is 0. As a very rough guide:

* With a score of thirty there is something woefully lacking in your motivation, so are you really ready to stop? Read Chapters 2 and 3 again, and think carefully about Chapter 8.
* If your score is fifty, you are half motivated, so think about why you want to stop. Concentrate on Chapter 8 particularly.
* With a score of eighty you are very motivated, so stopping should be relatively easy as long as you follow the three programmes carefully.
* If you score more than eighty, you should have stopped already!

But please don't give up hope if this little exercise tells you you don't really want to stop smoking. That isn't the purpose of the exercise. Remember, you can't succeed at anything until you know how much you want to succeed.

The aim of the questionnaire is to make you think about the issues – because something made you read this book, so some part of you does want to stop smoking.

This is called psychological reversal – you want to, and at the same time you don't want to. It might comfort you to know that almost everyone who attends an NHA Stop-Smoking Clinic suffers in exactly the same way. It doesn't mean that you won't stop smoking; it means that something has to be done about it. Some people stop painlessly – despite the addiction, the habit and the psychological dependence – because their motivation is strong enough. But more people fail. And lots of people stop smoking – but lots of people also start again.

As you read through the book you will learn where you went wrong before and what to do about it. By the time you start the Preparation Programme you will be going into something you *can* achieve. Then you will have found the motivation.

5

Good Habits, Bad Habits

IF BREAKING THE HABIT BREAKS YOU,
DON'T DO IT – CHANGE YOUR HABITS
INSTEAD.

Some questions answered in this chapter:

* How can I tell if it's habit or addiction that makes me smoke?
* Why is smoking the only habit I can't change?
* How do I stop using cigarettes as rewards?

The biggest habit of all

A lot gets said about smoking as a habit: 'That filthy habit', 'Break the habit', and so on. Doesn't that strike you as odd? Obviously, any habit can be changed if there is a good reason. And most people accept that smoking kills. So if smoking is just a habit, why don't more people stop doing it?

But smoking is not 'just' a habit. It involves both a habit and an addiction. And it is a habit like no other human activity. The more you do something, the more likely it is to become habitual. You go to work, eat meals, clean your teeth, drink cups of tea or coffee and so on. You are in the habit of doing these things.

How does smoking compare as a habit-forming activity? Let's compare smoking thirty cigarettes a day for twenty-five years with a number of other everyday activities:

$30 \times 365 \times 25 = 273,750$ cigarettes	cups of tea/coffee	54,750
	meals	27,375
	go to bed	9,125
	go to work	5,000
	feed the cat	18,250
	brush your teeth	18,250
	blow your nose	36,500
	get dressed	9,125
	wash the car	1,300
	TOTAL	179,675

No matter what activities you include, it is very hard to get them all to add up to the number of times you light a cigarette in the same timespan. That one habitual activity has been registered in your memory more times than every other habitual activity added together. It looks like a formidable habit to change.

Habit is defined as 'a behaviour pattern that has a degree of automatism', and what is so fascinating about it is that it is exactly as hard or as easy to change as we make it. A machine can be programmed to repeat a function again and again, indefinitely, but it can also be switched off. Unlike you, a machine cannot become addicted. Some patients in stop-smoking clinics think they will never change the habit; it is amazing to watch them discover that the habit is a pushover without the addiction.

Habit or addiction?

There are two keys to changing a habit. The first is deciding to do it – really deciding to do it, not wishful thinking. Habits don't change themselves. Something you have done more than a quarter of a million times is going to be the simplest thing in the world to keep doing. The second key is addiction. And frankly you are up against it if you try to change a habit of doing something you are addicted to.

This is a major reason why so many people make a complete hash of their attempts to stop smoking. It is sad to see smokers making all that effort to change their routine so as to avoid the habit, only to wake up in the morning and simply have to smoke before they can get moving. And as long as you smoke because of the habit, you will also trigger the addiction, because each cigarette demands the next one.

So the addiction won't let you change the habit, and the habit won't give you a chance to overcome the addiction. You're in a bit of a mess.

There is only one way to change a habit – you just change it (sorry, no miracle here). However, there are three ways to break an addiction. You can neutralize it (which takes medical treatment); you can wean yourself off it; or you can ignore it, which is usually called cold-turkey (although where turkeys come into this is a mystery).

To stop smoking successfully you are going to have to tackle habit and addiction together. They are mutually supporting, but this does not mean that they are the same thing. Addiction is a chemical response in the body, over which you have no control; habit is 'all in the mind'.

Don't let anyone try to fool you that addiction is 'in the mind'. Addiction is in the central nervous system (for our purposes, the brain), a physical organ subject to the same influences as all the other organs in the body. It has to be fed, just like your stomach, and it can be physically damaged, just like your heart or lungs. This 'all in the mind' stuff is something made up by psychologists.

Nicotine is a chemical. It has a chemical effect on your brain, and the human brain has no control over its own chemical status. The control you do have is in the mind, which is the data processing function of the physical organ called the brain. The brain is computer hardware, the mind is the software – they are separate but inter-dependent.

The effect of nicotine on the brain is like the effect of electricity on computer hardware. The program loaded into memory has no control over it, but is affected by it. Come what may, nicotine will affect your brain, and lack of nicotine will produce a withdrawal response. How you respond to that withdrawal will depend not on the hardware, but on the software – your psychological conditioning, your emotional dependence and your willpower. All these things are in the mind; they are, ultimately, under your control.

But isn't it interesting that, when you look at the list of habits above – or a specific list of your own habits – none of them would be difficult to change? Is this because of the smaller number of times you do these things compared to the number of cigarettes you light? Certainly that is a major factor; but equally important at least is the fact that no one ever became addicted to feeding the cat or washing the car. That is because none of these other activities has a chemical effect on the brain – they are non-addictive. You might think that eating is addictive for some people. This is not true; some people become psychologically dependent on eating, but that is quite different from addiction. And some people become addicted to certain foods (you might be surprised at how many foods are addictive) but they are not addicted to eating.

It is believed that some people can get addicted to jogging. That is not strictly true. What they are doing is becoming addicted to the endorphins (a type of hormone) produced when jogging. These endorphins are first interpreted by the brain as a reward, and then addiction sets in, so the runner keeps running to get the enjoyment from the endorphins, not because running in itself is addictive. It is the result of running, not running itself, that addicts.

Similarly, we could say that it is the result of smoking, not smoking itself, that is addictive. The lighting and smoking of cigarettes is a habit; the effect is addictive. You can become psychologically dependent on the activity, but the addiction is to the chemical effect on your brain.

In short, you are in the habit of smoking – but habit cannot be the reason you are unable to stop.

Don't 'break the habit'

You might have noticed that we don't talk in this book about 'breaking the habit'; we talk about 'changing habits'. Why is this?

If we say 'the habit', we are saying that smoking is the habit that makes you continue smoking. This is clearly nonsense. It is *a* habit, not *the* habit, no matter how deeply entrenched. It is one of many habits you have, but (we hope) it is the only one that involves an addictive drug. Always refer to it as *a* habit, and you will keep the habit part in its proper place.

More importantly, this entire programme is not about *breaking* a habit. It is about *changing* your habits. You will read in the Preparation Programme that if you can change your smoking habits – without even stopping smoking – you will learn to take control. Stopping smoking successfully is entirely about taking control. If you can control *when* you smoke, you are well on the way to controlling *if* you smoke. If you can say, 'I am in the habit of smoking now, after lunch, but I decide when I smoke – and today I decide not to, and I choose to leave it for another hour', you can control your desire to smoke. You will not use that control fully until you have completed the whole Preparation Programme, and dealt with addiction and the other issues. But when you do use it, you will succeed.

45

We have now answered these questions:

* How can I tell if it's habit or addiction that makes me smoke?

    Habit cannot make you smoke. Addiction makes you smoke. You become habituated and so you think it's the habit forcing you to smoke, but in fact it's the addiction.

* Why is smoking the only habit I can't change?

    You can always change a habit, unless you are also addicted. It is the addiction that makes the smoking habit so difficult to change.

6

Addiction and Dependence

DON'T LET ANYONE TELL YOU ADDICTION IS ALL IN THE MIND – DEPENDENCE IS, AND THEY'RE NOT THE SAME THING.

Some of the questions answered in this chapter:

* Why can I cut down to five or six a day but no further?
* What is the difference between my Addiction Threshold and my Addiction Level?
* How does dependence reduce my motivation to stop smoking?
* How do I control my addiction?

What's the difference between addiction and dependence?

Most people, including some doctors, fondly imagine that dependence and addiction are the same thing. The word 'dependence' tends to get used to cover both sides of the problem, but we prefer to differentiate clearly between addiction, which has a physical cause, and dependence, which is psychological. So from now on we are going to refer to dependence as psychological dependence.

Similarly, many people, and this still includes a lot of doctors, refer to something called psychological addiction. This is a mistake. Addiction should only ever refer to the

47

brain's physical need for a drug. For example, you might say you are addicted to Mozart, but this would not be correct.

Dependence is in the mind

One can enjoy the music of Mozart so much that to be without it is no fun. My teenage children might appear to be addicted to pop music, but what that means is that they like it an awful lot. And since we live in a society in which most of us can, within reason, have what we want, we feel deprived if we are prevented from having it. I should feel deprived if Mozart were banned, and my children would feel deprived if pop music were banned.

At a higher level, some people become obsessed. Football, for instance seems to dominate the lives of its fans, although it leaves others quite cold. Take a football fan's TV set away from him and you would be in serious trouble. He might become depressed, even aggressive, and would suffer something like withdrawal symptoms; but he could not be called addicted. He could, however, reasonably be called psychologically dependent. This is because his mental state depends, to some extent, on football. With it he is happy, without it he is unhappy. And this, as explained above, is caused at least in part by his expectations.

No matter what someone is psychologically dependent on, they can be weaned off it. Given the right support – perhaps some replacement for their dependence – and a good reason for doing it, most people can overcome such dependence.

An element of the psychology is that some people are more likely than others to become psychologically dependent. They have a poorer internal resource to cope with life, and are more susceptible to whatever makes life appear easier. Some children, for instance, are easily led, whilst

48

others are relatively self-sufficient. The ones who are easily led are more likely to succumb to peer pressure – they will, for example, start smoking under such pressure, whilst other children will find it easier to say no.

Given the narcotic effect of nicotine, anyone who finds life stressful is going to respond positively to smoking. And if life seems easier when you smoke, you have the beginning of psychological dependence. So is it fair, if we admit that nicotine helps a little with life's difficulties (and who has an easy life these days?), to expect people to overcome their dependence on it? We can only hope that you are not in a situation where you feel you are actually better off if you continue to smoke.

So much for dependence for the moment; we shall be coming back to it once we have looked at some aspects of addiction. Although dependence and addiction are separate entities, what keeps you smoking is the way they work together. Split them, tackle each of them in the appropriate way for the particular problem, and you will be in control. And, as we constantly assure you, with complete control you will be in a position to stop smoking.

Addiction is in the brain

Once you start smoking, you are almost guaranteed to get addicted.

* When you wake up, do you quickly have a strong need to smoke?
* When you smoke after a while without a cigarette, do you get a strong feeling of relief?
* Do you have more cigarettes in the first hour of the day than at any other time?
* When you are in a non-smoking environment, do you look forward to getting out so you can smoke?

* Do you stand outside, regardless of the weather, because you aren't allowed to smoke at home or work?
* Do you make sure you won't run out of cigarettes?
* When you try to stop smoking, do you get withdrawal symptoms such as mood changes, irritability, sweating palms, stomach cramps, headaches or any other abnormal physical symptoms?

If you can answer yes to any of these questions, you are addicted to nicotine. In fact the effect of nicotine on the brain is so powerful that your adaptation mechanism reacts extremely quickly, making you physically addicted within weeks – providing you smoke enough to trigger the mechanism. Some people only smoke one or two cigarettes a week, and could easily stop. They don't, because they don't feel it's worth bothering. Why don't they get addicted? The adaptation mechanism needs a fairly continuous dose of any drug to achieve adaptation and then maintain it.

Many smokers find they can exercise enough willpower to cut down to about five or six cigarettes a day, but no further. They simply cannot understand why this is. This amount of smoking gives you enough nicotine to maintain your addiction, and is called the Addiction Threshold. As long as you smoke that many you will remain addicted, because your adaptation mechanism is still working. Try to cut down even more, and you immediately challenge your addiction.

So your brain is fighting to maintain its addiction, regardless of what you want. This proves an immensely important point: no matter how much you want to stop smoking, you will have to overcome the addiction. This means that you will withdraw from nicotine, and the resulting symptoms will be entirely outside your control.

The degree to which you will experience these symptoms ranges enormously. Some people have very strong symptoms, while for others they are so slight as to be unnotice-able – though this is not as common as some 'experts' would have you believe. For thousands of patients whom we see in our clinics, the withdrawal symptoms have been enough to stop their previous attempts to stop smoking.

So at this point let us destroy another myth. Willpower does not overcome addiction: it overcomes the *effects* of addiction. If you are addicted to nicotine, withdrawal symptoms of some kind are inevitable. Whether you over-come them depends on two factors – how bad they are, and how much willpower you have.

And now, while we are exploding myths, let's take a look at another one. It is commonly believed that heavy smokers are more addicted than light smokers. This is absolutely not true.

The reason is simple. As explained above, you need about five or six cigarettes a day – and no more – to maintain your adaptation. But the average smoker gets through about twenty a day. So clearly you don't smoke twenty, thirty or whatever because of any physical craving – it must be for other reasons. You are addicted because your body has to maintain its adaptation to the poison; your body has no interest in nicotine, tobacco or cigarettes beyond that point.

The Addiction Threshold and Your Addiction Level

Although all smokers have a similar Addiction Threshold, each smoker has a specific Addiction Level. Despite this, smoking at the Addiction Threshold will satisfy the ad-dictive craving. How is this apparent contradiction ex-plained?

The challenge to your addiction happens at a particular level – the Addiction Threshold – but the way your body maintains its adaptation is specific to you. Cars offer a simple analogy. A 7-series BMW has a huge petrol tank, but a Mini has a very small one; both cars, though, need only a trickle of petrol to start their engines. The BMW's tank is so big because of the consumption of the engine, but most of the 100 litres the tank contains is irrelevant to the trip to the supermarket. BMW drivers only challenge their car's fuel tank by driving hundreds of miles.

Like the BMW, your body is equipped in a way that satisfies your needs (to remain adapted to the poison). On a day-to-day basis, however, that complex machinery will not be needed. You only challenge your adaptation mechanism when your tobacco consumption drops below the Addiction Threshold. Once it does, the Addiction Level becomes important, because it is this that determines your ability to remain adapted to the poison.

Over the years you have smoked, your body has been using its adaptation mechanism to enable it to absorb a highly poisonous substance, nicotine, taken in by an extremely unpleasant delivery method, burning gases. It only does this because of the narcotic effect of nicotine and, once you got on to the merry-go-round of smoking, because of the psychological pressure to continue smoking. But how did you adapt to the poison in the first place?

Whilst the mechanism of adaptation is the same for everyone, each person's ability to deal with any challenge to their health is different. This is one of the major failings of high-technology medicine; it treats everyone as a standard model. A fifteen-year-old girl who has only ever smoked the occasional cigarette, a fifty-year-old man who smokes eighty a day, and a seventy-year-old woman with emphysema all have the same adaptation mechanism, but clearly they each have a unique response to the challenge of smoking.

Similarly, everyone has a unique response to all the challenges that life throws at them, a response which depends on a huge range of factors including age, sex, weight, physical health, mental health and current medication. The same flu virus does not affect everyone in the same way – some suffer more than others, and some people who have been exposed to the virus do not react at all.

When you started smoking, your body was faced with an extremely serious challenge. You had the same adaptation mechanism as other people, but the result of the adaptation process will have depended on a wide range of factors like those listed above. At some point, your adaptation mechanism succeeded in meeting the challenge. How far it had to go was individual to you, and it is what we are calling in this book your Addiction Level. (The NHA's doctors call it the Endpoint of the addiction, and they use it to make up the neutralizing neutrogen in the correct concentration for patients. A full explanation of this process, and of how the NHA learned to neutralize addiction, is given in Chapter 17.)

The Addiction Level is your body's own response to the challenge imposed by absorbing a toxic substance called nicotine. Once it has met that challenge (if you like, once it has worked out a means of absorbing the poison), how many cigarettes you go on to smoke is irrelevant. The Endpoint has been established – you have adapted to the poison. That is the adaptation your body will fight to maintain for as long as you are a smoker. Whether you smoke five or fifty a day will not change it. And when we refer to how addicted you are, this is what we are saying.

Addicted or dependent?

You are both. In the same way that many smokers think that the number of cigarettes they smoke determines how addicted they are, a lot of smokers believe that the number of years they have smoked influences how addicted they are.

This is not true. Once you are addicted, that's it – the Addiction Level depends on your immune system's response to the poison. Once your body had adapted, the addiction is complete. If you go on to smoke for fifty years you won't get any more addicted – but you will become more dependent.

Now we have seen what the difference is between addiction and dependence, let's take a look at how dependence works to keep you smoking and, ironically, how it keeps you addicted. And how addiction works to keep you dependent. Once you understand how the two conspire to keep you smoking, you will be able to separate them and deal with them individually, so that they lose their combined power.

Dependence makes you believe in habit

Smoking is a habit, but the habit doesn't have the power to make you smoke. Your *belief* that habit can make you smoke is proof that you are psychologically dependent. Habit, by definition, can be changed at will. If you really wanted to stop smoking, you would accept that you can change any habit.

So the effect of psychological dependence is that it makes you believe you cannot change your habits. This reduces your motivation to stop smoking.

Dependence makes you afraid of failing

There are very few things you attempt in your life that are critically important. Many things seem so at the time, like your driving test, or someone you have just fallen in love with, or a house you desperately want to buy. With hindsight, almost nothing is critically important.

People attach an inordinate importance to succeeding

54

when they attempt to stop smoking. If you have smoked for thirty years, whether it takes one day or one month to stop is completely unimportant.

Because you are so dependent on smoking, you believe in failure, and you fear it. This reduces your motivation to stop smoking.

Dependence makes you afraid of succeeding

If you are dependent on smoking, clearly you will be afraid of stopping, as much as you want to in your more rational moments. Fear of succeeding is an excellent way to fail. The slightest problem that crops up is enough to stop you trying any longer. In our clinics we sometimes see patients who obviously don't want the neutrogen to work for them. What they are doing is coming along to the clinic, not using the neutrogen as prescribed, and continuing to smoke. 'Failing' with the neutrogen is all the excuse they need to smoke for the rest of their lives. They say to themselves, 'I tried, but obviously I am an impossible case.' There is no such thing.

Fear of succeeding clearly reduces your motivation to stop smoking.

Dependence makes you smoke when you are stressed

Although nicotine does have a narcotic effect, we know that on balance smoking makes life more, not less, stressful. Because you have experienced the transitory nature of the narcotic, you believe strongly in the ability of smoking to help you deal with life's stresses. In your more rational moments you might accept that the stress imposed by smoking outweighs the narcotic effect, but you are rarely that rational when you have not smoked for three days.

Since the benefit of smoking is imaginary, we can reasonably say that this is an aspect of psychological dependence. This can cause you to fear life without the support of cigarettes.

This fear reduces your motivation to stop smoking.

Dependence makes you fear the loss of enjoyment

There is an element of enjoyment in smoking, but it is illusory. If you didn't enjoy the first cigarette you ever smoked, you also won't enjoy a cigarette after not smoking for a week. Therefore smoking is not enjoyable – but you *believe* it is, and that belief is enough for the enjoyment to become real.

If you really wanted to stop smoking, why would the enjoyment of smoking make you continue? Isn't that a complete contradiction? Yet we see a large number of patients who simply can't explain this contradiction. The answer isn't difficult. If the enjoyment of smoking is greater than the desire to stop, you won't stop.

Unless you break the myth. If, after a week's abstinence, your next cigarette isn't enjoyable, this is all the proof you could want that you don't really enjoy smoking. You think you do, and that is called psychological dependence.

It is certainly enough to reduce your motivation to stop smoking.

Dependence makes you believe that smoking keeps you occupied

Many smokers simply cannot imagine never smoking again – not necessarily because they are afraid of this situation, but because smoking has become such a major part of their daily routine. Smokers commonly use lighting up as a reward, or to punctuate a boring job. You have perhaps come to depend on smoking in these situations, but it almost goes without saying that the dependence is all in the mind.

The belief that you need cigarettes will reduce your motivation to stop smoking.

So why are you dependent?

This is the big question. If the reason you cannot stop smoking is addiction and dependence, and if dependence means it is all in the mind, why can't you change your mind? Wouldn't this solve half the problem?

Because the addiction won't let you.

Exercise

Imagine you have some habit which fits very roughly with smoking. Let's take chewing gum. You might say:

* I enjoy gum.
* I like to hand gum round in company.
* I chew gum when I'm bored.
* I allow myself gum as a reward.
* I like to chew gum after a meal.
* Chewing gum can help me relax.

Some years ago, it became known that a substance which people were in the habit of using every day was the cause of a massive amount of sickness and death. Just image that that substance was gum, and it was killing three hundred people a day, a lot of them children.

Is it conceivable that for most users the benefits of chewing gum would outweigh the danger? Would gum chewers say, 'I really want to stop but I can't, because I always chew gum after a meal. Don't remind me that it's going to shorten my life.'

Naturally, in these circumstances, gum would be banned by the government, because there would be no profit for them in it. Either that or they would tax it, and if they taxed it so that it cost over £800 a year to chew gum most people would stop buying it anyway, because, frankly, no one needs to chew gum that much.

And that is the point. No one *needs* to chew gum. They can have all the same habits with gum as with tobacco, and all the same associations with pleasure. What they don't have is the *need*. And there is only one thing that makes people need tobacco.

Addiction.

In that case, why does dependence keep me smoking?

On its own, it would seem that no matter how psychologically dependent you were on smoking, you would be able to overcome it. This raises two questions to which we must find answers:

* Why can't you overcome psychological dependence on smoking?
* Why don't you become psychologically dependent on other things?

The reason these two questions go together is that the answer to the second gives us the answer to the first.

We said earlier that some people become dependent to the point of obsession on watching football. But even this dependence is nothing like dependence on smoking. No other dependence, not even dependence on gambling, is like dependence on smoking. The reason is one of stunning importance: there is nothing else you do which involves an addictive substance that makes you psychologically dependent. That is why you can't overcome the psychological dependence on smoking – or, more accurately, that is why you became dependent on smoking in the first place.

This leaves one more question:

* Why does an addictive substance make users psychologically dependent, if the two aren't connected?

Well, they aren't exactly connected, because they have different roots, but they do influence each other. They form a defensive circle, but also a vicious circle: a defensive circle because they protect each other, and a vicious circle because they can only satisfactorily be beaten if they are separated, and this is not easy.

Within a week of starting to smoke seriously, you are addicted – your brain is then prepared to fight to maintain its adaptation to the poison. It is perfectly natural that your perception of the addiction will be that you need the addictive substance (which you really do). Where this becomes a problem is when you are no longer addicted – but you still believe you are. The addiction will have gone, even without medical treatment, within a week, but it is totally unrealistic to expect the mind (as opposed to the brain) to recognize this fact in such a short time.

The psychological dependence on smoking takes a lot longer to get over than dependence on anything else, because of the addiction. The addiction plants in your brain a very powerful message that you must smoke. Even when that message is no longer valid, the memory of the message remains, and it is a message of fear.

Addiction, dependence – and motivation

Now we come full circle, because we have said that anyone who wants to stop smoking enough will do so. They will overcome the withdrawal symptoms until the addiction is dead. They will work through the dependence until they are in control. But they will only do these things if they want to do so *enough*.

But what does 'enough' mean? What is enough for one person will not be enough for another. You have your own specific Addiction Level, your own dependence issues, each with its own degree of severity, and your own motivation level. So what you actually have is a three-sided problem:

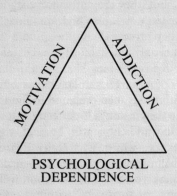

PSYCHOLOGICAL
DEPENDENCE

If you had enough motivation, the addiction and dependence would not matter so much. If you were less dependent, you would not need so much motivation. If you were less addicted, you might be less dependent. And so on.

It is very difficult to assess motivation. You should already have completed the Motivation Questionnaire in Chapter 4, so at this point you will have a good idea of your score. But motivation is profoundly affected by ability. Once you have read this book with all the enthusiasm with which we have written it, you will be in a very strong position to tackle your psychological dependence. Once you have done that, at least enough to put yourself in control, you can tackle the addiction. At that point you can see you would have little difficulty stopping smoking; but you have got to get to that point.

In our clinics we cheat. We control the addiction medically, and this has the most remarkable effect: it motivates people to stop smoking. Those who come to us for the right reasons seriously want to stop but cannot because they are addicted, and because the psychological dependence is too great. They have failed to stop before, and they are fed up, resentful, angry and hostile. They have enough motivation to come to the clinic, but they are almost daring us to fail them (which we don't, because we don't know the meaning of the word).

So our patients are in control of the addiction from the first day of their programme. The next morning they can wake up and not need to smoke, and starting the day without a cigarette is a marvellous incentive to go on. You almost certainly smoked first thing this morning, so you do not have this advantage. That is why this book works the other way round. By following the programme correctly, you will deal with the psychological dependence first. This is slower than at our clinics, but the end result is the same.

At some point, which will probably take a while, you will have got your smoking down to five or six cigarettes a day. You will have achieved this by changing your habits, getting to grips with your stress response, changing your attitude to enjoyment and so on. You will then be at a decision stage.

At that point you have to deal with the addiction, which means one of three things:

* You can ignore it because the withdrawal symptoms will not affect you in the same way they did before – because you will have completed the Preparation Programme and you are now in control. (You are not trying to handle stress and habit and all the other obstacles while suffering withdrawal symptoms.)
* You can get help with the withdrawal symptoms through acupuncture or hypnosis.
* You can get medical treatment – the neutrogen.

61

We have now answered these questions:

* Why can I cut down to five or six a day but no further?
  You need this many to satisfy your addiction. When you cut down, you change your habits and do other things which you can control. Your body needs five or six a day to satisfy the addiction, so naturally it will start to withdraw if you try to go below this number. You cannot control your addiction, so you get involuntary symptoms when you reach this level. This scuppers your attempt.

* What is the difference between my Addiction Threshold and my Addiction Level?
  Your Addiction Threshold is the point at which your body starts to withdraw because it is getting insufficient nicotine. For most smokers this is five or six cigarettes a day. Your Addiction Level, however, is unique to you, and is a measure of the way your immune system responds to nicotine. It would concern an NHA doctor if you were being prescribed the neutrogen, because it is your body's response to the drug. Knowing the difference between your Addiction Threshold and your Addiction Level enables you to appreciate that your degree of addiction is unaffected by how many you smoke, or how long you have smoked for.

* How does dependence reduce my motivation to smoke?
  If you are psychologically dependent on smoking, you are living a lie. This means you don't *need* to smoke (unless you are still addicted) but you still think you do. As long as you are dependent, you will fight your own desire to stop smoking. The only answer is to deal with these dependence issues, because they are all under your control. Use the Preparation Programme to achieve this.

* How do I control my addiction?

    Once you have worked through the Preparation Pro-
    gramme, you will have greatly increased your ability to
    overcome withdrawal symptoms with the Cessation
    Programme. If this is still not possible, you can try
    acupuncture or hypnosis. If these don't work for you,
    ask your GP about Addiction Neutralization Therapy.

7

Analyse Your Problems

The purpose of this questionnaire is not to discover whether you are psychologically dependent, because you already know you are. Its purpose is to assess the relative importance of each issue for you, which is why each section is scored out of 10. Knowing the relative importance of each aspect is vital because of the way the Preparation Programme is structured. It works by helping you first to separate out the different problems associated with stopping smoking, and then to deal with them one by one so that you won't be overwhelmed.

The psychological issues are all those which are not physical, and the only physical issue is addiction. You might think that the irritability you suffer when you try to stop smoking is psychological, but it isn't. It is an emotional response to a physical trigger – lack of nicotine. This might sound confusing but don't worry about it, because we are going to list for you the psychological issues. Just remember that:

* Anything you worry about *before* you stop smoking is likely to be psychological dependence.
* Any symptoms that occur only *after* you have not smoked for a few hours or days are likely to have a physical trigger, i.e. addiction.

Questionnaire

Tick in the space provided.

Stress (Chapter 9)
Q1
Have you ever restarted smoking because you came under stress?
Yes ...   No ...

Q2
Do you smoke more when you are stressed?
Yes ...   No ...

Q3
How stressful is your life, whether work or domestic?
Not at all ...   Slightly ...   Quite ...   Very ...
Impossibly ...

Q4
If you were faced with an extremely serious situation, once you are a non-smoker, would you light a cigarette to help?
Yes ...   No ...

Q5
Once you are a non-smoker, do you think you could resist the temptation to smoke even though you are highly stressed?
Yes ...   No ...

Habit (Chapter 5)
Q6
How difficult do you think it is going to be to change your smoking habits?
Not at all ...   Slightly ...   Quite ...   Very ...
Impossibly ...

Q7
How difficult do you think it is going to be to cut down the amount you smoke (regardless of whether you might increase again later)?
Not at all ... Slightly ... Quite ... Very ...
Impossibly ...

Q8
Have you found the habit difficult to change before?
Yes ... No ...

Enjoyment (Chapter 8)
Q9
Overall, how much do you enjoy smoking?
Not at all ... A little ... Quite a lot ... A lot ...

Q10
How many of the cigarettes you smoke do you enjoy?
A few only ... Half ... Most ... All ...

Q11
Which cigarettes do you enjoy most? Tick one only.
First of the day ... After a meal ...
When relaxing ...

Q12
Can you imagine a time when you no longer enjoy smoking?
Yes ... No ...

Fear of failing (Chapter 10)
Q13
Have you failed before?
Yes ... No ...

Q14
Have you succeeded before (for at least a year)?
Yes ... No ...

Q15
Are you afraid of failing this time?
  Yes . . . No . . .

Q16
Do you think this is your last chance?
  Yes . . . No . . .

Fear of success (Chapter 10)
Q17
Can you easily imagine never smoking again?
  Yes . . . No . . .

Q18
Does the thought of never smoking again worry you?
  Yes . . . No . . .

Q19
Does the thought excite you (even if it worries you as well)?
  Yes . . . No . . .

Social (Chapter 8)
Q20
Do you mix with smokers socially?
  Not at all . . .   A little . . .   Quite a lot . . .   A lot . . .

Q21
Can you imagine mixing comfortably without smoking?
  Yes . . . No . . .

Q22
Can you imagine drinking without ever smoking?
  Yes . . . No . . .

Your score

First, work out your score for each of the answers.

Q1
Yes = 1,   No = 0

Q2
Yes = 1,   No = 0

Q3
Not at all = minus 2
Slightly = 0
Quite = 2
Very = 4
Impossibly = 6

Q4
Yes = 1   No = 0

Q5
Yes = 0   No = 1
TOTAL FOR QUESTIONS 1–5 (stress) = . . . (maximum 10)

Q6
Not at all = minus 2
Slightly = 0
Quite = 2
Very = 3
Impossibly = 4

Q7
Not at all = minus 2
Slightly = 0
Quite = 2
Very = 3
Impossibly = 4

Q8
Yes = 2   No = 0
TOTAL FOR QUESTIONS 6–8 (habit) = . . . (maximum 10)

Q9
Not at all = minus 2
A little = 0
Quite a lot = 1
A lot = 2

Q10
A few only = 0
Half = 1
Most = 2
All = 3

Q11
First = 0
After meal = 1
Relaxing = 3

Q12
Yes = 0   No = 2
TOTAL FOR QUESTIONS 9–12 (enjoyment) = . . .
(maximum 10)

Q13
Yes = 2   No = 0

Q14
Yes = 0   No = 2

Q15
Yes = 3   No = 0

Q16
Yes = 3 No = 0
TOTAL FOR QUESTIONS 13–16 (fear of failing) = . . .
(maximum 10)

Q17
Yes = 0 No = 3

Q18
Yes = 4 No = 0

Q19
Yes = 0 No = 3
TOTAL FOR QUESTIONS 17–19 (fear of success) = . . .
(maximum 10)

Q20
Not at all = 0
A little = 2
Quite a lot = 4
A lot = 6

Q21
Yes = 0 No = 2

Q22
Yes = 0 No = 2
TOTAL FOR QUESTIONS 20–22 (social) = . . . (maximum 10)

What your score means

You can now see which of the issues is most important for
you, which you must take into account when formulating
your stop-smoking programme. Your success at stopping
smoking will depend on your success at eliminating each of
your problems. If your biggest problem is that you socialize

a lot with other smokers, and are reluctant to give up this pleasure, now is the time to recognize that you are dependent on the pleasure of smoking socially. No one has a cure for this. Like everything else in this programme, the answer lies within you – understand what the problem is, and decide to deal with it.

None of the problems highlighted in this questionnaire is impossible to overcome. Read through the relevant chapter in the book that relates to each section of the questionnaire until you understand why it is a problem; only this understanding will enable you to make the necessary changes.

8

The Pleasure of Smoking

THE PARTY HAS TO END SOME TIME, BUT HAS IT REALLY BEEN SO GREAT?

Some of the questions answered in this chapter:

* Why don't I enjoy *all* the cigarettes I smoke?
* Will I be able to enjoy going to the pub again if I don't smoke?
* What will I do after meals when I no longer smoke?
* Why do I enjoy smoking even though I want to stop?
* Why is it I hated smoking at first but now enjoy it?
* Will I ever stop enjoying smoking?

Most smokers who want to give up admit they enjoy smoking. This is a terrible conflict; it would be bad enough trying to overcome an addiction to something unpleasant, but smoking is not unpleasant. Or is it?

Think back to the first time you ever smoked – probably an illicit cigarette when you were a teenager. The chances are, even now, that you remember thinking it was foul. It might have made you feel sick or dizzy; you will have coughed – the human throat was not designed to swallow the smoke from burning tar. However, you persevered, because you had a good reason for wanting to smoke. What started as an ordeal became bearable, and then it became pleasant (it didn't become necessary until somewhat later).

And now you enjoy smoking. What happened between

the coughing and spluttering stage and the 'I enjoy smoking and I don't care if I do die of lung cancer, I've got to go some time' stage? It is not habit. Habit is the *result* of continual smoking. It is Addiction that is the *cause* of continual smoking. Habit will not lead you to believe in the enjoyment, but addiction does.

This is not to say that the enjoyment is a figment of your imagination produced by your addiction. Once learnt, smoking really is enjoyable – or rather, the immediate *result* of smoking is enjoyable. The physical act of smoking in the sense of drawing poisonous gases through your throat into your lungs is *not* enjoyable – it is simply the mechanism by which the narcotic effect of nicotine can be enjoyed. But do it a quarter of a million times and the poor old brain is deluded into thinking it is the cigarette you are enjoying.

So what? you might well ask. Enjoyment is enjoyment. The point is this. You have learnt to believe that the enjoyment you get from smoking comes from smoking itself. It does not: it comes from the drug contained in the cigarette. If you can get used to the idea of separating the activity from the result, you are on the way to under-standing how to stop enjoying smoking. And that is pre-cisely what you are going to have to do.

We all know the old chestnut about enjoying not banging our head against a wall; as a statement it is obviously silly, but then the opposite is even sillier. What it means is that not until you stop banging your head against a wall do you appreciate how comfortable *not* banging your head against a wall can be. Similarly, while you are a smoker you have no idea how good being a non-smoker might be. It is just possible that if you stopped you would suddenly realize that, whilst you thought you enjoyed it, not doing it is actually ten times better.

Some cigarettes are better than others

Think about the cigarettes you smoke through the day. Do you enjoy *all* of them? Probably not. As you go through a day's smoking make a list of those you particularly enjoy, those you quite enjoy, and those that you just smoke but don't know why.

And now answer this question. Do you enjoy smoking, or do you enjoy smoking sometimes? The chances are that you really enjoy smoking sometimes, and those times are likely to include:

* First thing in the morning.
* With a drink.
* In a social setting.
* After a meal.
* Relaxing after a hard day.

Now if you enjoy smoking, say, after a meal, it is not actually smoking that you are enjoying but smoking after a meal. In other words, the meal is an important element in the enjoyment of that particular cigarette. Take the meal away, and it is not your after-dinner cigarette but just any old cigarette.

The idea is to split the enjoyment into its real causes. To do so, you need to understand exactly what it is you are enjoying.

Look at it like this. You might currently say you enjoy smoking after a meal. Imagine that your meals consisted of no more than dried pellets taken in a space capsule whizzing round the Earth. Do you think such a meal would trigger the desire to smoke? Almost certainly not (of course space capsules are no-smoking areas, but you take the point).

So now you have to face up to the fact that it is not actually smoking that you enjoy, but that something triggers you to smoke, and your response – smoking – is

75

enjoyed. That trigger could be any of the events we just mentioned, like a meal. Let's look now at each of them, try to understand why they are triggers, and why enjoyment is the result of your response to the trigger.

First thing in the morning

In our clinics we often ask people which part of their smoking 'habit' they are going to find hardest to break. Typically they will say it is the first one in the morning.

There is a lot of misunderstanding about this first cigarette of the day. The reason you enjoy it so much is not habit (habit, almost by definition, does not actually produce pleasure because it is something you do automatically). Neither do you wake up and think, 'You know, what I would really enjoy now is a cigarette.' You smoke that first one because the level of nicotine in your body has dropped so drastically that you need to top it up, and quickly. So that first one of the day can be crossed off our list of enjoyment cigarettes.

With a drink

Most smokers agree that when they have a glass in one hand, they have a strong need for a cigarette in the other. Perhaps this cigarette really is enjoyed. But then perhaps not.

Question – does the cigarette make the drink more enjoyable, or does the drink make the cigarette more enjoyable? Do the drink and the cigarette make the company more enjoyable, or does the company make the drink and the cigarette more enjoyable?

It's very unlikely that you can answer this question. But it will help if, next time you are in a social setting and people are standing around drinking, you take a look at those who are smoking, and then at those who are not. (If you are caught out staring at an attractive member of the opposite sex, just say you are conducting important research.)

Are the drinkers who are smoking enjoying themselves more than those who are not? Conversely, are those who are not smoking enjoying themselves less than those who are? It is extremely unlikely that you will be able to detect the slightest difference.

The reason you enjoy a cigarette with a drink is that you associate the two. And the reason you associate the two is habit. People in pubs smoke. You smoke in the pub. Therefore you enjoy yourself more when you smoke in the pub. And now you are in the habit of smoking in the pub, and you enjoy yourself in the pub, so you must enjoy a cigarette when you're having a drink.

It's somehow logical, but this doesn't make it any more sensible. The fact is, a cigarette is no more enjoyable with a drink than at any other time. It seems as though it is – but that's just the effect of brainwashing. Now that you know it isn't really true, you can start to work at breaking the association. You have got to convince yourself that you can enjoy a drink without a cigarette.

There is no special trick; the important thing is to keep reminding yourself that it is only a habitual association – not an association you are forced to keep making. There is no real connection between drinking and smoking, other than that you remember you have always done it. So this is a habit, not a real need, and habits can be changed.

The main reason people fail to change their habits is that they believe the habit controls them – they refuse to accept responsibility for changing the habit, because it isn't easy. Ask yourself if you accept responsibility for changing the habit. Or are you letting the habit control you because it is easier than taking control? If you are really honest with yourself, you will probably have to admit that you have tended to take the easy option. Now you have to take control.

After all, you want to be a non-smoker, don't you? So why would you want to smoke?

In a social setting

A large part of the enjoyment of smoking in a social setting comes from the association between smoking and drinking, which we have just demolished.

Another part is the fact that other people are smoking. Of course, a lot of them will not be smoking, because social settings are increasingly less smoky than they used to be. But there will probably still be enough people smoking to remind you that you would enjoy a cigarette.

Why do you enjoy a cigarette more when other people are smoking? Probably for two reasons. The first is that we are herd animals: we like to do what other people are doing. You could argue that, since the majority are not smoking, the herd instinct should make us copy them instead. But not doing something is never going to inspire as much imitation as doing something. So seeing people around you smoking is naturally going to encourage you to smoke.

The second reason is more interesting. You are a smoker, and you need to smoke at regular intervals because you are addicted to nicotine. It takes very little indeed to trigger the desire for a cigarette, because there is an underlying desire all the time. The slightest thing will make you light up, and being with other smokers is ample.

We started by saying that you enjoy smoking in company, but perhaps what we are saying is that this is not actually the reason you smoke in company. You need to smoke, you receive a trigger (other smokers), you respond to the trigger. Responding to a trigger will always be interpreted by the brain as enjoyment.

There are two stages in overcoming this trigger, or 'enjoyment' as you have been calling it. In the short term you stop exposing yourself to the trigger – for as long as possible you stop socializing with smokers. (You might feel this is too high a price to pay – in which case you are wasting your time trying to stop smoking, and you might as well give this book to someone who will make better use of it.)

Having removed the immediate trigger and given yourself some breathing space, the next task is to undo the brainwashing. Read this section again, and really understand this issue. You used to think you enjoyed smoking in company, but this turned out to be a myth, didn't it? You could continue to 'enjoy' smoking, but why would you?

After all, you want to be a non-smoker, don't you? So why would you want to smoke?

After a meal

The reason you want to smoke after a meal is mostly the same as the reason you want to smoke with a drink. It has become a habit.

But for many smokers there is another reason, too. Apart from those people who have to smoke during a meal itself, most smokers are going without nicotine for perhaps half an hour, an hour or even longer. The nicotine level in the body drops considerably in an hour. If you smoke twenty a day, your body is used to getting a fix roughly once or twice an hour. If you don't smoke – whether it is because you are in a non-smoking environment or because you are eating – you will certainly be ready for one as soon as possible.

What we have here, therefore, is both habit and need. You will have to work backwards on this, because you had a need first (lack of nicotine), so you smoked after meals; and you developed a habit as a result. The habit will need to be undone first, in the same way as your association

79

between drinking and smoking. You have to learn to take control, because habit is always within your control, and that is one of the most important lessons you are going to have to learn.

An easy way to control this particular habit is simply to extend the time between finishing your meal and smoking. Leave it just half an hour. What you will find is a strong urge to smoke, because of the habit, but satisfaction when you finally light up.

Habits are never really just broken. You could say they are always replaced, because if you change your habits you are actually creating new ones. For example, not smoking after a meal is a habit.

So replace your habit with a new habit. If nothing else, this demonstrates that you can do whatever you want, because habit is always under your control. This will leave you with the original problem – if you don't smoke for an hour, your body is going to start asking you to.

That is addiction, which is dealt with in Chapter 6. All we want to say here is that this is the time to stop believing the myth about having to smoke after a meal. You could, of, course, give in to the habit, and let it control you. You could have just one at that time, because that is the one you really do enjoy. Or you could take control.

After all, you want to be a non-smoker, don't you? So why would you want to smoke?

Relaxing after a hard day

Have you ever experienced that unique pleasure of smoking a cigarette after a long day at work, or after finishing a particularly difficult task, or simply after struggling home from the supermarket? Probably thousands of times.

This is the pleasure of reward, and it is quite normal to reward ourselves in these circumstances. Tobacco, however, gives us a unique kind of reward, although alcohol is similar. The main difference is that for most people intake of alcohol is restricted both by time of day and frequency. But there is no limit to when or how often you can reward yourself with a cigarette.

Yet again we have to break down this particular use, as we did with after-dinner smoking and smoking with a drink. And as with these, not only do you have a reason for smoking in this way, but you have become used to doing it. You needed or wanted to smoke as a reward, you got used to getting the reward – in other words, you created the habit.

So, yet again, the way out of this situation is gradually to change your habit. You are in the habit of rewarding yourself with a cigarette when you finish a job, so the first step is a small change – leave the cigarette half an hour, so you are still getting your fix, but you are breaking the close association between effort and reward.

Surprising as it may seem, this association is not entirely psychological. There are two potential physical reasons why smoking is used as a reward.

The first is that nicotine is a psychoactive drug – a narcotic; you could almost call it a 'recreational' drug. Particularly after expending mental energy, nicotine can give you a lift. Curiously, if the expenditure of energy has left you mentally stressed, nicotine can do the opposite by tranquillizing you, depending on how you use it (see page 91).

Whichever of these two uses applies to you, you will get a direct and rapid chemical effect from a cigarette, and this 'pleasure' is a very obvious reward. You will be conditioned to expect that 'pleasure' when you feel you need a reward, rather like a laboratory animal is conditioned to get a reward for performing the task desired by an experimenter.

The second kind of physical reward comes because, if you have been engaged in some task during which you cannot smoke, you will have started to withdraw from nicotine. Remember, your body is used to getting its fix at least once an hour if you smoke twenty a day, so when a job is finished it will be looking for nicotine. This is not the sort of withdrawal experienced when you actually try to stop smoking; it is very low-level withdrawal which you do not notice consciously, but which keeps you smoking all day, every day.

Getting that fix is simply going to be interpreted in your brain as reward. In crude terms, abstention equals craving, unsatisfied craving equals withdrawal, withdrawal demands fix, fix stops withdrawal, and the brain interprets the end of withdrawal as pleasure.

What all this means

What we have been doing so far in this chapter is to look at what you yourself describe as the enjoyment of smoking. You might say that you enjoy smoking generally, but this is true of very few smokers. Most would have to admit that they enjoy smoking more at some times than at others. As soon as they say this, they have to realize that their enjoyment depends on the situation, not just the cigarette. Those situations fall into just two categories.

The first category consists of the situations we have been looking at so far, which are typically first thing in the morning, with a drink, in a social setting, after a meal, and relaxing after a hard day. In each of these cases, it is the situation which partly creates the enjoyment. Remove the situation and, by your own admission, you remove the enjoyment.

To stop smoking you need to undo the concept of enjoyment. To achieve this, you must recognize the 'enjoyment' situations and do something constructive about altering them.

In the second category there are times when you enjoy a cigarette, and yet you could not say that the enjoyment is situation-dependent. The best example is of course the first one in the morning. As we have just seen, this is not enjoyment in the same sense at all. It is need. You need to smoke, and you enjoy the satisfaction of that need.

At other times during the day you just enjoy a smoke. In each of these cases, if you really analyse it, you will find that what you are doing is satisfying a need. By doing so you are, in a way, creating enjoyment. However, it is not enjoyment in the sense of a hearing beautiful piece of music, spending a weekend in Paris or even consuming a hot salt-beef sand-wich. Remember, the delivery method of this enjoyment is burning tar smoke down your throat – something which you found awful the first time you tried it. So it is, by definition, not enjoyable. The enjoyment is something you have come to believe in for a number of reasons, none of them connected with burning tar smoke down your throat.

So what are these needs that smoking satisfies, and then makes you believe it is enjoyable?

The first is obviously addiction to nicotine. And while you are addicted to any substance you will always interpret the satisfaction of your addiction as pleasure, regardless of the reality of the delivery method.

Then there is stress. Smoking is used universally to handle stress. Within seconds of getting a shot of nicotine in the brain, you are more relaxed. So potent is this effect that the interpretation of it as enjoyment is inevitable. The nicotine tranquillizes, and tranquillity has to be felt as enjoyment.

There are other needs that smoking satisfies which might be specific to you, but these two, addiction and stress, cover most of them. The important question for you now is this: are these real needs which smoking satisfies, or have you created them yourself? Or even worse, has smoking itself created the needs? The short answer is that non-smokers don't have the needs – at least, they don't have needs that only smoking can satisfy – so we have to come to the unfortunate but inevitable conclusion that these needs are created because you smoke. You thought that smoking was fulfilling your needs, instead of which it turns out that smoking is creating the needs and then fulfilling them. Crafty, isn't it?

And to go back to our earlier point, by satisfying these needs you are interpreting smoking as enjoyable. So you started smoking, then you developed needs which only smoking could satisfy, then you came to believe that the enjoyment which resulted from satisfying these needs stops you giving up smoking.

Most smokers say they enjoy smoking, and we have seen that, whatever the reasons, this is true. But what we have also seen is that it is smoking which creates the situation where you don't want to give up the enjoyment.

At this stage ask yourself a very important and rather interesting question. Do non-smokers enjoy themselves? Of course they do. To say that all smokers enjoy their lives more than non-smokers do would be nonsense. And yet there are millions of smokers saying they cannot stop because they enjoy it. That is not the reason at all.

If smokers admit that they know smoking is likely to make them ill and shorten their lives, they need a much stronger reason for continuing than enjoyment. Yes, they enjoy it in a way, but the enjoyment is not the reason they cannot stop. They think it is, but they are mistaken. If life is as enjoyable for non-smokers as it is for smokers – and it is almost certainly more enjoyable because they are healthier and richer – the reason enjoyment stops smokers giving up is that what is interpreted as enjoyment is not actually an obstacle but an excuse. Genuine though the enjoyment might be for you, why do you need to use it as a reason for not being able to stop smoking?

Because you have to continue smoking. Because you are addicted. Because you have no other means for dealing with stress. And because you are therefore psychologically dependent. What you are not is dependent on the enjoyment, so stop using it as an excuse right now.

We have now answered these questions:

* Why don't I enjoy *all* of the cigarettes I smoke?

    Because enjoyment stems from the satisfaction of low-level craving, you will enjoy those cigarettes more which satisfy the greatest need. Many of your cigarettes are smoked simply out of habit, and this brings no 'enjoyment' because the need is missing. This proves that you don't actually enjoy smoking, otherwise you would enjoy all of the cigarettes you smoke.

* Will I ever be able to enjoy going to the pub again if I don't smoke?

    Non-smokers enjoy themselves in the pub at least as much as you do, so all you need to do is become a non-smoker. The bit you might not enjoy is the time it takes to break the association between the pub and smoking, but it is breaking this association that actually brings back the enjoyment of going to the pub.

* What will I do after meals when I no longer smoke?

    The washing up! From the perspective of a smoker, after meals looks like one cigarette you won't want to give up. That is the addiction talking. You will be learning to break this association *before* you actually stop smoking with this programme, so you will prove this to yourself before it can become a problem.

* Why do I enjoy smoking even though I want to stop?

    As much as you want to stop, the addiction has to be fed. Each time you feed an addiction of any kind you experience pleasure, because you satisfy a craving. And also because nicotine is a narcotic drug.

* Why is it I hated smoking at first but now enjoy it?
    Smoking is, by definition, unpleasant. It only becomes
    pleasant once you are addicted to the nicotine it
    delivers. You do not enjoy smoking, but you do enjoy
    the result – your fix.
* Will I ever stop enjoying smoking?
    As soon as you break the addiction, which takes a few
    days. Some people don't even enjoy their early morn-
    ing cigarette, which is the proof that it is the drug, not
    the cigarette, that you enjoy. But you will remain
    psychologically dependent on smoking for a long
    time, and this will make you believe you would still
    enjoy it. If you try smoking after a week, you will not
    enjoy it, but you might persevere until you do! What
    you are afraid of now is not that you will never stop
    enjoying smoking, but that you *will* stop enjoying it,
    and this feels like too much to lose.

9

Taking the Stress Out of Smoking

IF STRESS MAKES YOU SMOKE, YOU ARE
GOING TO HAVE TO DEAL WITH IT. SO DO IT
NOW.

There are two distinct ways to approach this subject.

The first is to for you to get to work on stress. This is going to help you stay off cigarettes, and it is also going to help you live the rest of your life.

The second is for you to accept that no amount of smoking is going to make your life less stressful. Smoking simply does not help you deal with stress. On the other hand, it would be wrong to say that the help you believe you get from smoking is entirely an illusion. The help you have got over your smoking career has convinced you that you need to smoke to cope with life. This is psychological dependence.

When you were a small child you could not have imagined coping in the big wide world without your parents; unsurprisingly, you do. Don't allow yourself to believe that anything is essential for your survival, because nature made you perfectly capable of surviving with what you have.

When *Homo sapiens* evolved it had all the biological means to survive in the world, and did so for tens of thousands of years without tobacco. You were not born a smoker, and it is fairly unlikely that you started smoking because of stress. So stress does not make you smoke –

rather, you smoke because, if you did not, you would be stressed. This is entirely different and is, you will agree, a kind of dependence; you didn't need to smoke for stress when you were a non-smoker, but you do now you are a smoker. Don't you find that rather suspicious? And a little sad?

How you develop stress-related dependence

Stage 1
You are not stressed. You are smoking your usual amount, say one cigarette every fifty minutes. This is a natural rhythm which you have subconsciously established to keep you free of nicotine craving – every drug addict has a craving/relief cycle, even if it not a conscious one.

Stage 2
A stressor occurs. Assuming it is at least thirty minutes since your last shot of nicotine, a cigarette at this point makes you feel better, partly because your inhalation method is long, which provides enough nicotine to have a narcotic effect (see page 91), but also by relieving unrecognized craving. Your brain interprets this feeling better as stress relief – the stress would be even worse if you were also craving your drug.

Smoking also replaces up to fifteen per cent of the oxygen in the brain with carbon monoxide, which will increase the deadening effect.

Stage 3
If this process occurs frequently enough, you subconsciously learn to relieve stress by going through this craving/relief process. The more you do it, the more you feel the benefit.

Stage 4

Because you are now dependent on the process of relieving low-level craving to relieve stress, combined with the effect of the drug itself, you experience anxiety if the drug is not available when a stressor occurs. The only way out of this predicament is to adopt a new mechanism to replace nicotine.

No matter how old you are, you retain from childhood the need for someone or something to comfort you in times of stress. As a child it was your mother or a teddy bear. Now it is cigarettes. You grew up and no longer needed your mother. You can stop needing tobacco.

Understanding stress and stressors

Stress is your response to stressors. Stressors are, in themselves, not harmful – at least not in the way you think of. When you learn to drive, you are stressed; this is the fear that you will do something wrong and crash. The fear itself is not harmful, but a crash would be; so, assuming you don't actually crash, the fear is worse than the actuality.

In this case stress is unnecessary. No one has been hurt, but worrying about the possibility has caused stress. Of course there are times when stress is necessary, like when a close relative is seriously ill. Or perhaps not. There is an old adage that worrying never solved anything, and it is true. You will naturally worry greatly in this situation, but will it help? In fact, not only will it not help but it will make matters worse, because the effects of stress on you will reduce your coping ability.

If by stress we mean distress, it can be seen that stress is always unhelpful and unnecessary. It doesn't help you to cope, and coping is what you need in the face of stressors. So, if stress is always a bad thing, why do we have a stress response at all? The answer goes back a hundred thousand years, when *Homo sapiens* lived in an entirely different world.

Sabre-tooth tigers and mammoths roamed the planet, and man had to compete for food; food was in fact man's greatest priority, as it still is in very primitive tribes who have a similar lifestyle to our prehistoric ancestors. Faced with a sudden threat of imminent death from something large and hairy, the only response was either to attack it or to run like hell. It is what is called the 'fight or flight response'. The body suddenly produces adrenalin, which stimulates the heart and raises blood pressure. The whole body, brain and all, works better and faster, ready to fight to the death or escape. When faced with a huge and hairy beast, it is an entirely appropriate response.

But when faced with a recaltricant child, a gas bill or a car that doesn't start it is an entirely inappropriate response. Unfortunately our bodies don't know that we are living in the twentieth century, because they haven't evolved fast enough. Evolution takes place over hundreds of thousands or even millions of years – much more slowly than lifestyle, which in the Western world has developed immeasurably since the industrial revolution and again since the Second World War.

So as far as our bodies are concerned we are living in an alien world. People respond to twentieth-century situations as if they were cavemen, because their adrenal glands have not developed since then. Most of our work in the NHA is about the health implications of adaptation to modern life, from maladaptation to the poor quality of our food to the structural damage caused by asking our bodies to adapt to sitting, which we were not designed to do. Producing adrenalin all day to cope with frequent challenges of a minor nature is something we are not adapted to, because our adrenal glands were meant to cope with infrequent challenges of a life-threatening nature.

Nicotine – stressor or sedative?

What is the relevance of all this to smoking? First, smoking has an effect on this stress mechanism. It raises blood sugar levels and promotes the production of adrenalin. In other words, it stimulates your stress response. But paradoxically it is also a narcotic – it slows brain activity. So at the same time as relaxing you it is stimulating you. You can actually use nicotine in two opposite ways; a short puff on a cigarette will supply enough nicotine to the brain to stimulate it, but a long drag will have the desired narcotic effect. When you are tired you will take short puffs, and when you are stressed you will take long drags, and you do this instinctively, without knowing you are doing it.

So you use your smoking, or more accurately your access to nicotine, to regulate your stress response. But you use it badly, because of the paradoxical nature of the drug; and because of the addictive nature of the drug you are now stuck with a dependence on it to control that very stress response. Because of this dependence, stopping smoking will actually reduce your ability to cope with stress in the short term. The critical point is that non-smokers cope with stress just as well as smokers, so you can be sure that, once that dependence is overcome, you will handle stress just as well as before.

In fact, without the additional stressors imposed by smoking when you are trying not to, you will be less stressed.

Is smoking the best way to manage stress?

As long ago as 1963, an internal memorandum from a tobacco company lawyer read, 'We are, then, in the business of selling nicotine, an addictive drug effective in the release of stress.' One of the NHA's doctors is fond of telling patients that nicotine is such a good sedative that it would be prescribed but for the fact that it kills three hundred people a day.

So clearly, even if it has a therapeutic effect in some ways, nicotine is completely inappropriate as a tranquilliser. So you have to make a choice. If you want to stop smoking, you have to do two things:

* Accept that no matter how good nicotine has been for tranquillizing you in the past, the cost grossly outweighs the benefits.
* Find something better.

Is there something better than nicotine?

On the basis that nicotine comes packaged in tobacco, and tobacco is going to shorten your life, the answer has to be Yes. But let's forget that point for now, and look at the question in another way. Is there anything you could use that would help you to deal with stress in the place of nicotine?

First you must come to terms with a fundamental truth. You are habituated to using the drug you are addicted to for handling stress. Nothing else is going to have the same appeal at this stage, and nothing else is going to work as well as long as your memory is searching for your drug. Nevertheless, if you really want to stop smoking, and stress makes you smoke, what choice do you have?

There are many drugs which will help you to cope with your life just as well as nicotine, if not better. Heroin will take your problems away, for example. You don't use heroin because it is a dangerous addictive drug. You use nicotine *despite* it being a dangerous addictive drug; the difference is that you are already addicted to nicotine, so it is your drug of choice, but it could just as easily have been heroin.

92

So somewhere out there there must be something (let's assume for the moment a drug) which will help you to cope with life. In all seriousness, look for something you can use instead of nicotine which will help. Put it this way; imagine you had never heard of tobacco, and you went to your GP for a tranquillizer. He offered you a prescription for a new drug called tobacco. You happened to ask if there were any side-effects, to which he replied, 'Some.'

'What do you mean, "Some"? Has anyone been made ill by it?'

'Yes, quite.'

'Quite ill, or quite a lot of people?'

'Both, actually.'

'Well, how ill? And how many people?'

'Very ill, I'm afraid.'

'Don't tell me someone has died.'

'I'm afraid so, quite a few.'

'You mean you want me to use a drug that has killed people? How many people?'

'Well, in this country, about three hundred people a day.'

'I beg your pardon?'

Bizarre, isn't it? The reason you use tobacco is not because it is an appropriate drug, but purely and simply because you are addicted to it. Even when the addiction is broken, you will remain psychologically dependent on it for stress management for years. There you have it. You actually believe that a drug which is going to shorten your life by ten to fifteen years is a good way to handle stress. Almost any other drug would be better, although we assume you would choose one that is legal.

Is there a drug-free way to handle stress?

Of course there is, but everyone wants a quick fix. Narcotic drugs were used in the most primitive societies, and why not?

There is still a general belief that tobacco is a reasonable way to handle stress, and given that you are dependent on it this makes it difficult for you to consider the alternatives.

If you accept that your aim is to be a non-smoker, you have no choice but to look for some other means to control your stress response. In our clinics we have two techniques, only one of which can be taught in this book. The other is a form of shiatsu, which is tremendously effective. It can be taught, once your correct acupuncture points have been located, in a few minutes. If you get the chance, try to find someone who can teach you to do this.

The technique that we *can* teach you in this book is so obvious that you would never have thought of it. We have discussed how you produce adrenalin to deal with a stressful situation (a stressor), which means that adrenalin is in fact your stress response. Ideally, if you could control the production of adrenalin you could control your stress response. In other words, no matter how bad the stressor, you would control how you respond to it, which is direct stress management.

You can affect the working of your adrenal glands by the way you breathe. Unless you have been trained in breathing techniques, the chances are that you habitually do what is called costal breathing – expanding the chest only. This is exactly what happens in a fight or flight response, so it is clearly associated with stress.

The opposite of costal breathing is diaphragmatic breathing. This is associated with a resting state, when you are not producing adrenalin. It is deeper and more effective, the effect being to slow down your responses. Paradoxically, even if think your job requires you to respond quickly, this kind of breathing actually gives you more control, allowing you to be more decisive and to take controlled action. These are the very things you need when faced with stressful situations.

It is not difficult to learn diaphragmatic breathing. Follow these instructions:

1. Put one hand on your chest and the other on your abdomen, and take a very deep breath. Your chest will expand and your abdominal muscles will contract. This is what you are going to learn *not* to do. Breathe out.

2. Leaving you hands where they are, take a deep breath again, but this time consciously push your abdomen out. Your chest will take care of itself – once your abdomen has expanded, keep breathing in and you will feel your chest expanding as well. The effect is to allow your diaphragm to drop a little, giving your lungs more room to expand and thus increasing your intake of air.

3. Breathe out as fully as you can, pushing in hard with the hand that is on your belly. As long as your abdomen goes in and out in the right order, you are breathing diaphragmatically.

Keep breathing!

Once you have mastered this simple technique, all you need to do is practise it so much that you use it automatically. This sounds impossible, but if I can do it so can you. Practise for two minutes at least four times a day. Every time you stop – at traffic lights, the sink, your desk or the supermarket queue – ask yourself whether you are breathing diaphragmatically. It might take months to achieve good breathing, but it will be the best thing you ever did for your health after stopping smoking.

When you come under serious stress as a non-smoker, you are going to remember the help that cigarettes used to give you. But altering your stress response *now*, and training yourself to control it, is going to make a tremendous difference when that stressor hits you. Controlled breathing is the most effective and immediate stress management technique you will ever learn.

Prevention is better than cure

There is also another simple technique to learn, called preventive stress management. Do it now, and do it from time to time for the rest of your life.

Take a piece of paper and draw a nice big barrel on it. A barrel is designed to hold a finite amount of liquid, and not a drop more. A barrel filled to the top is stressed, but an overflowing barrel is distressed – it cannot do its job. You have a finite capacity to contain stressors without responding (or overflowing), and the barrel makes an excellent visual symbol.

Leave the piece of paper lying around, and every time you think of a stressor that bothers you, write it in the barrel. The secret lies in being both honest and comprehensive. Stressors are not just the obvious things like money, relationships, jobs and health. It is important to include the smaller things, like a bill you could pay but put off, a DIY job you never do that causes you aggravation, even a child asking for help with a school project. You will find the small stressors are things that could be dealt with quite easily, but get left because you are too stressed by bigger problems.

The key to reducing your stress load is not the major stressors over which you feel, probably correctly, you have no control. It is those niggling problems which occupy too much space in your subconscious and bog you down. Get rid of them.

Go back to your barrel a day or two after you have included every possible problem. If a rain barrel has a tap at the bottom, turning it will allow the barrel to release some of its existing water rather than overflowing at the top. The tap in your barrel represents the small stressors, because they are easy to deal with. So leave the harder problems and give time to some of the smaller ones which you thought were unimportant. Then, lo and behold, the level in your stress barrel will go down. This leaves more room for those stressors which have to stay, and your barrel – your stress capacity – does not overflow. It may sound too simplistic to help, but it really works.

This simple technique is an important part of the Preparation Programme in Part Two, so try it now. And don't forget that it's a very useful exercise to go through again from time to time, long after you have stopped smoking.

A fatal mistake

The most common reason for going back to smoking is stress. And yet built into this simple statement is a terrible error on the part of smokers. When under extreme stress you might smoke, despite everything you have learnt from this book, but please read this next part very carefully, and keep it in mind always.

If you smoke one cigarette, or even two or three, you will calm down. But if you keep smoking *after* you have calmed down, you will become readdicted. *Even if you get desperate, never smoke enough to become readdicted.* That is your responsibility. Smokers think that once they have had one cigarette they might as well continue. This is untrue, and please don't ever forget it.

10

Great Expectations

STOP TRYING TO SUCCEED ALL AT ONCE.

Some of the questions answered in this chapter:

* Is my smoking my own fault?
* How do I know when I've failed to stop?
* How do I know when I've succeeded?
* What's the point of cutting down?
* Why can't I stop thinking about cigarettes when I stop smoking?
* Does stress make me smoke?

Almost everyone who tries to stop smoking underestimates the task. They expect to succeed, and to succeed immediately. The conventional wisdom is that you have to choose your moment, then stop dead and just forget you were ever a smoker. But this idea, as we have explained, is naive.

This sort of misinformation is put about by those doctors who would like to believe it is true because they have no other answer. Time and time again we see patients who say their GP told them simply to stop, as if such advice were some sort of miracle cure. If anything it is arrogant and patronizing, and smokers resent it.

Another group of people who tell you simply to stop is ex-smokers. 'You don't need any patches or other gimmicks, I just woke up one morning and decided I'd had enough, so I stopped, there and then, mind you I can't say I don't fancy one now and then, wouldn't it be nice if I could be a social smoker but I can't, I know I couldn't trust myself, it's been ten years now and not a week goes by when I don't feel tempted, you ask my wife, mind you she's been trying for years, got no willpower, spends a fortune trying to stop, you should hear her coughing of a morning, blather-blather-blather . . .' If you are being troubled by a smug ex-smoker, ask them to read page 199 of this book. It will help them to understand your problems and should enable them to sympathise with you more.

The fact is that some smokers can stop easily, and some can't. And since you are reading this book the chances are you have had difficulty stopping, so you are not one of the lucky ones.

The result of all this well-meant if clumsy advice is that, when you finally have a real go at stopping, anything less than immediate and absolute success is seen as failure. But forget that idea and just put the whole thing into perspective.

1. You are currently dependent on a drug as addictive as heroin. Would you expect a heroin addict to stop 'just like that'?
2. You have smoked for a long time. How many years is it? Do you seriously expect to be instantly able to stop something you have been doing for that length of time?
3. You have been using nicotine as a tranquilliser and probably as a stimulant as well. Are you suddenly going to be able to do without that tranquilliser, and the stimulant, just because you decided to stop smoking?

Stop blaming yourself

With all the pressure to stop, you are left with the belief not only that you should do it, but also that it is your fault if you can't. Let's look at this idea, because you almost certainly do believe it's your fault.

The NHA Stop-Smoking Clinics questionnaire includes the following question:

Who do you blame most for your inability to stop smoking?
A. Doctors, the tobacco industry, government.
B. Yourself.

Which would you tick? If you are like 99 per cent of patients, you would blame yourself. Now let's see if this is reasonable. Try to think back to when you first smoked. The reason you started was almost certainly that someone either gave you a cigarette, or at least put the idea into your mind. Almost all young people who start smoking do so because of peer pressure.

The reason you persevered, despite your strong distaste for tobacco, was the pressure not to give up – because if other people enjoy it, it must be good. (This is a fascinating contradiction – your own intelligence was telling you it was awful, but you were determined to enjoy it because other people did!)

It takes as little as a week to become addicted to nicotine, so while you were still desperately trying to get used to being a smoker, you were already addicted. So now you were smoking, not because you wanted to, but because you had to.

You were not to blame for trying cigarettes – you were under pressure to do so. You were foolish to give in to the pressure, but foolishness is part of the human condition. You were not to blame for being determined to overcome the difficulty of smoking, for the same reason. And you were not to blame for becoming addicted. That is the fault of the drug.

No one told you, all those years ago, that smoking would shorten your life, would drastically reduce your spending power, and would one day make you a social outcast, did they? You are not the culprit in your smoking problem – you are the victim.

And if you are the victim, just who *is* to blame? Think about it. Who makes the cigarettes? Who sells them? Who taxes them? Who tells you to stop smoking but has no way of helping you? Now do you know who is to blame?

So for goodness' sake, stop blaming yourself. Start to think of yourself as a victim. You have been had. You are spending a great chunk of your income on something you don't want, you know is going to shorten your life, and you feel guilty about. You think you are stupid for doing it, don't you? If the answer is Yes, then read the the last few paragraphs again, because you aren't. At all times, while you are trying to stop smoking, say to yourself, 'It is not my fault, I am not stupid, I have been fooled into becoming a drug addict and I am trying to do something about it.' You might want to add, 'With a fat lot of help from anyone else.'

As long as you blame yourself, you aren't going to have a lot of patience with yourself. And you are going to need a great deal of patience because stopping smoking is big. Not frightening, not impossible, but still big.

Stop believing you are a failure

None of this is intended to put you off trying. In our long experience in clinics, smokers have shown repeatedly that they have failed not because they can't stop smoking, but because they were expecting too much, too quickly. So at this point let's define what we mean by a 'big' problem.

We could, with some justification, say that stopping smoking is easy. After all, if you were locked in a cell you couldn't smoke. If you had no money at all, and no friends to cadge from, you couldn't smoke. If your hands were tied behind your back you couldn't smoke. And if you

102

had some serious disease of the mouth you couldn't smoke.

What this means is that if the ability to smoke were outside your control, you would not be able to do it. The reason you *can* do it is precisely because it *is* in your control. Given that you are a rational human being, you should be able to exercise enough control to stop smoking. That you cannot do so is testament not to the impossibility of stopping smoking but to your own lack of control.

So what we mean by 'big' is not 'horribly difficult' but 'complicated'. And we have spent some time explaining it because you have got to stop thinking in terms of success and failure. Anyone can stop smoking – *everyone* can stop smoking. Recognize that success is available to you, but that it is going to take time, effort and understanding. If you have difficulty stopping smoking, don't give up trying.

So many people fall into the trap of thinking that unless they are immediately successful they have failed. They haven't failed, they just haven't succeeded yet. The task is simply going to take longer than they thought.

Just imagine that you are trying to stop smoking right now. Let's say you normally smoke twenty a day. In the last twenty-four hours you have struggled with a desperate craving but you haven't given in to it, and you finally go to bed praying that tomorrow will be better. But tomorrow is worse, much worse. You wake up wishing you were dead. You cannot possibly face the day without a cigarette. Finally you cave in – you dash to the corner shop and smoke like there's no tomorrow. Before you know it you've smoked three – you're sitting at the kitchen table with a cup of tea and seventeen cigarettes left in the pack. You light another. It's not that you would normally have four in half an hour, but you need to make up for lost time. Sixteen left in the pack and the whole day ahead of you. You might as well smoke that day, and try again tomorrow. At this point you are a hundred per cent failure.

103

Start believing in cutting down

Now let's look at another scenario. All right, so you go and buy a pack. But cigarettes come in tens as well as twenties. Why buy twenty? Ten is more than enough to avoid disaster. You get home having smoked two. Now *wait*. You wait because you must give your body time to get the 'benefit' of the two cigarettes. Sure, you have a cup of tea, but now you are exercising some self-control, so you don't light up the third one. Of course, you don't have to exercise self-control – you can smoke instead. That's entirely up to you. You are the one who wants to stop smoking. And if you really do want to stop, why would you light the third one? Now the battle commences. Light it, and you've given up trying. Don't light it, and you're in control.

If you don't light it you've passed the test. Let's imagine the rest of the day. You don't smoke any more that morning, but you have one with your afternoon cup of tea, and one that evening. Is this failure? If you had smoked a pack of twenty you would have been a hundred per cent failure, but you only smoked four. You reduced your smoking that day by eighty per cent. Well done.

Now a spoilsport will tell you that what you have managed is no good – either you stop smoking or you don't. If you smoke at all you are a failure. This is rubbish. We are talking about one day, not the rest of your life. Cutting your smoking by eighty per cent cannot conceivably be regarded as failure.

Would you expect a child to walk as soon as it learns to stand, to run as soon as it can walk? So why do so many people insist that smoking four cigarettes means failure? Frankly, even a twenty per cent reduction is better than nothing, but almost any smoker could reduce their consumption by fifty per cent at a stroke if they were serious about it. As explained earlier, you need only five or six cigarettes a day to maintain your addiction, so to cut down from twenty to ten is not as difficult as you think. To cut down from forty to twenty is even easier – it just takes thought. It doesn't even take a lot of effort – just thought. And the thought is this: stop trying to succeed instantly.

Start exercising self-control

Imagine you are a forty-a-day smoker. Wouldn't it be nice to be a twenty-a-day smoker instead? You would probably agree that it is easier to stop smoking if you are a twenty-a-day person than if you are a forty-a-day person, so there is definitely some point in cutting down like this. And by the same token there is some point in cutting down, if you currently smoke twenty, to ten. It isn't the end of smoking, but it *is* the beginning of the end. It means you are taking control, instead of smoking controlling you. With control you are in a position of power.

If you can demonstrate to yourself that you can control your smoking, you will believe in your eventual success. But by saying to yourself, 'If I've smoked one I might as well continue', you are just demonstrating that you have no serious intention of stopping smoking.

Now imagine that you have shown this self-control and halved your smoking. And imagine that you keep at the same level for several months. You are on the way to becoming a non-smoker, but instead of being one of those people who are forever stopping and starting you are in control, you are halving the damage to your health and you are saving a lot of money. Well done.

What you may be thinking at this stage is that it is not possible to cut down your smoking like this because it will simply go up again. Let's examine this idea. Is it true, or is it a myth?

If you tried cutting down before, and found that you did

indeed gradually increase again, think now why this happened. There were probably two reasons. The first would have been that you were stressed, and you believed you needed to smoke to deal with stress. The second would have been that you couldn't see the point of keeping your smoking down anyway. This was because you had been brainwashed into believing that you should either stop completely or not at all.

From now on, even if the same thing happens, remember that there is always a point in reducing the amount you smoke. Remember that *some* success is always better than none. Nothing breeds success like success.

The problem is that failure breeds more failure.

Stop allowing yourself the luxury of failure

If you stop smoking for six months you will feel great. You are a winner. And if you then give in momentarily you are suddenly a failure. This is what some experts try to make us believe, anyway. They say you are only a success if you stop smoking for a year or more. How silly this is – a heavy smoker would probably be delighted to stop smoking for six months. If you stop smoking for six months, you are at that point a success. One day's smoking, or even one week's smoking, doesn't make you a failure.

If you have a temporary lapse, you are only a *temporary* failure. The critical thing is to come to terms with what has happened and to accept that the failure is temporary. You could even say it is not a failure at all, because as long as you really want to stop smoking, and are prepared to continue working at it, how can you be a failure? You just haven't succeeded *yet*.

This belief that temporary failure equals total failure is one of the most depressing myths in the whole business of stopping smoking. Don't ever be fooled into believing it.

Why do so many people believe in failure at this point? Remember that all the time you are trying to stop smoking there is a little devil inside your head trying to persuade you to start again. You are constantly in conflict with yourself – you want to stop but you are psychologically dependent, so you always harbour a small hope that you will fail.

Most smokers subconsciously hope for failure because they can then say, 'I've really tried. I really did want to stop smoking, but I failed. It's obviously impossible for me to stop, so I'm just making life harder by trying.' Have you ever felt this way?

If you have, you can see how easy it is to believe in failure. And one cigarette, or even a whole day's cigarettes, can be enough to make you believe you have failed. Giving in to failure is easy. Anyone can do it. The point is, though, that you have not failed – you may not have succeeded, but you have not failed either. You have not failed until the day you die, and if you stop smoking the day before you die, you succeeded.

And this brings us very conveniently to the question of what exactly success means.

How do you know when you have succeeded?

At the moment you have a desire – to stop smoking. But what does this mean? How do you define your target? Stop smoking for ever, or just for the next twenty years? If it is indeed only twenty years (and you really wanted to stop for ever) will you have failed? Obviously, twenty years as a non-smoker cannot be called failure – but what about ten years, or five? It is common for people to stop for five years and then start again, but few of them would say after four years and eleven months that they had failed to stop smoking. Even after they started again, they would probably say they had stopped successfully for five years but then started again.

Your target is to stop smoking for ever, but there will be a point at which you would accept you have succeeded. When do you think that will be? After one year, two, three? If you are a heavy smoker (forty-a-day or more), six months might look like a long time.

Similarly, how do you define failure? Logically, you have failed if you haven't achieved your target. But we have a problem here. Your target is to stop smoking for ever, and yet we have just agreed that twenty years, even though it is not for ever, would be considered success. And so would ten years, or five, or perhaps even one.

So now you need to ask yourself an interesting question. How do you know when you have failed? Confusing, isn't it?

The point is that you cannot actually define failure, so stop believing in it. You have only failed when you give up trying to succeed. And you stopped trying to succeed in the past because you thought you might as well.

Apart from the obvious practical reasons, the reasons people fail when trying to stop smoking are:

* They don't know how to, because no one tells them.
* They set impossible targets, because our national culture is built on reward for success, instead of support.

At NHA Stop-Smoking Clinics our culture is one of support, rather than targets. Our patients know they will be supported indefinitely, so worrying about success and failure is pointless. Even if they start smoking again, they haven't failed: they simply start the programme again, and succeed again. Despite all this, we get depressed at the number of times we encounter patients who cannot make this cultural change.

Mrs M. from Essex came into our London clinic, and was shocked when the neutrogen actually controlled her craving to smoke – within half an hour of the treatment she was bubbling with excitement because her addiction was suddenly under her own control. Two days later she smoked seven cigarettes, and she smoked between five and ten a day after that. Why?

She made the mistake of believing that a forty-a-day smoker for thirty-six years must stop in one day. And when the psychological dependence overcame her willpower, and she smoked, she gave in to failure. She did not need to smoke that many – three or four a day would have been enough – but she gave in to the luxury of failing.

On the other hand, as we said earlier, even ten a day is a seventy-five per cent reduction from forty. It took extended telephone counselling to persuade Mrs M. that she had not failed. She kept saying, 'Oh, well, I'll try again.' That was nonsense. She didn't need to try again, because she was succeeding. Other people had let her down before, and she expected us to do so now. It takes some patients a long time to accept that we aren't going to do this. The reason we don't, when perhaps others would, is that many so-called experts in stopping smoking are geared up to regard anything less than immediate success as failure.

After thirty-six years of being a heavy smoker, it was going to take more than three weeks for Mrs M. to become a non-smoker. With the control over her addiction achieved by the neutrogen, and with a new attitude, she did indeed go on to become a non-smoker. But it took four months of learning to look for success, not out of a bottle or packet, but within herself. Mrs M. thinks we performed a miracle – but we didn't: we just helped her to achieve what had always been possible.

Learning from your attempts

The chances are that you've tried to stop smoking before and failed. What lessons do you feel you learned from that failure? The most likely responses are that you yourself were to blame for your failure, you are a failure yourself, you are no good, you have no willpower, you are stupid and everything is your fault – none of which is likely to be true, and you probably know it in your more rational moments.

It's just possible that it wasn't your fault. And, in any case, where does fault come into it? Since you almost certainly underestimated the difficulty of overcoming the addiction, and received little formal instruction in habit changing, and were given no expert help with handling stress, and quite possibly got little or no support from those who should have helped you, you would seem to have learnt entirely the wrong lessons.

Exercise
Take a sheet of paper for each attempt you have made to stop smoking. Write down the reasons why you failed in each case – or for going back to smoking after you had succeeded, to put it correctly – whether it was very short-term success (days or weeks), or for quite a while (months or years). Let's guess what your reasons were, and suggest the lessons you might learn from them.

Bad temper/irritability/inability to concentrate

REASON: These are withdrawal symptoms, over which you had no control.

YOU THOUGHT you were weak-willed, because you believed you should have been able to control them.

LESSON: Recognize the symptoms (see pages 123–4), and accept that they are inevitable. Decide before you try to stop smoking what you are going to do about withdrawal symptoms, but don't get caught out by them.

110

Withdrawal, and how you deal with it, is covered in detail in Part Two.

You couldn't get cigarettes off your mind

REASON: When you stop smoking after many years you don't suddenly forget about it, much as you would like to. You are practising what is known as the wishful thinking method of stopping smoking.

YOU THOUGHT you were never going to forget about smoking, and that you were quite likely to be taken away by men in white coats.

LESSON: You were expecting too much, too quickly. You were probably in conflict, because you were afraid of success and/or failure. Stop putting yourself under pressure. If it helps to have a pack of cigarettes handy, allow yourself to. Don't believe the myth (which you might have created yourself) that this will make you smoke. The main reason you will smoke at this point is pressure – the pressure you have created yourself.

You couldn't get over the habit

REASON: You know by now that habit is a reason for continuing to smoke, but it is not a reason for not being able to stop. Since you didn't understand that the habit was under your own control, you made no serious attempt to do so. You might have convinced yourself that you couldn't change your habits, but you would have been lying.

YOU THOUGHT that the habit was keeping you addicted.

111

	Naturally, you were wrong – what was keeping you addicted was the addiction.
LESSON:	First, come to terms with being responsible for your habits. Second, stop confusing habit and addiction. You can change your habits without help, but addiction will take more. Third, having accepted responsibility for your habits, do something about them (see the Preparation Programme in Part Two).

You needed to smoke in a social setting

REASON:	You have, quite naturally, always associated socializing with smoking. This might be no more than a habitual association, or you might consciously feel that smoking is a prop in a social setting.
YOU THOUGHT	that this was a habit you would never break. If you were using a cigarette as a prop, you might also have believed you would not be able to cope in company without one.
LESSON:	There are two separate lessons, because there are two possible problems.

If it is an association problem it is quite difficult to break. You really do believe a glass in one hand means a cigarette in the other. But take a look at drinking, socializing non-smokers – do they have a cigarette in the other hand? No, so the association is not a fact of life but is personal to you. Logically, then, you could become one of those non-smokers who don't make the association. This lies within your control, so don't make the

112

mistake of thinking it is impossible.

The second potential problem is that you cannot manage in company without a cigarette. This may well be true. However, the problem won't be removed by any known stop-smoking therapy, so you are going to have to face up to it. Recognize that your problem is not that you cannot stop smoking but that you lack self-confidence. At this point ask yourself a question. You want to stop smoking, but you need cigarettes to deal with being in company. Are you going to tackle the issue of self-confidence, or are you going to continue smoking? Now is the time to stop fooling yourself. Reread Chapter 9, which looks at the stress angle, and decide to do something about it. Always deal with the real problem – in this case cigarettes are not the issue, stress is.

And now a thought to destroy the myth of needing to smoke in company. When you go out, say to the pub, who are you socializing with? The chances are that most of the company consists of old friends. And you can't have a drink and a chat with friends you've known for years unless you have a cigarette in your hand? You've been kidding yourself. It's an excuse.

You were fine until you came under stress
REASON: Stress didn't make you smoke. It can't have done, because stress doesn't make non-smokers smoke. What made you

smoke was the *belief* that you needed to smoke to cope with stress.

YOU THOUGHT   that smoking even a single cigarette would help. You were wrong.

LESSON: The first lesson is that smoking doesn't remove stress. When are you going to learn this? Why is it so hard to learn? It's because, for as long as you are addicted to nicotine, you will believe in the power of the drug. But even when you have overcome the addiction you won't suddenly learn the lesson. You will have years of conditioning to undo – but believe us when we say that you will, one day, realize that smoking was not decreasing your stress but increasing it.

The second lesson is what just one cigarette does. It gives you perhaps a 50–50 chance of becoming a smoker again. The reason is that all the time you were trying not to smoke you were in conflict with yourself – wouldn't it be nice if you could have just one? As soon as you smoke just one, the memory of perhaps a quarter of a million cigarettes comes flooding back – and the overwhelming memory is of pleasure (because addicts 'enjoy' their drug). If you smoke just a few more, you will regain the adaptation you fought so hard to lose, by which we mean you will become addicted again.

You were afraid of your success

REASON: Many would-be ex-smokers are afraid of succeeding, but this fear doesn't just go away once you have succeeded (if we count success as short-term). In fact, immediate success can have an unfortunate effect: it sometimes makes people realize just how much they were secretly hoping to fail – they have succeeded almost against their will. We see this in our clinics, because the neutrogen stops the addiction so quickly. This removes the excuse of the addiction, which raises the paradoxical problem of unwanted success. The patient is then faced with issues he or she was perhaps unprepared for.

YOU THOUGHT that you might have made a mistake – perhaps you were wrong about wanting to stop? Perhaps you were not ready? Perhaps it was a bad time to try? Perhaps nothing.

LESSON: Recognize that addiction and dependence are self-sustaining; by definition they fight for their own survival. Remember that dependence means you *think* you are still addicted, even when you no longer are. Think of dependence as your addiction's last line of defence.

At this stage you are primarily worried about the thought that you will never smoke again. Just a moment, though – this is what you wanted, isn't it? Why is there a conflict? The conflict arises because you only *thought* you wanted to stop; the desire to stop was in conflict with the addiction. No one's desire to stop is 100 per cent. Realize that what you are fighting is not your doubts about stopping, but the drug itself and the dependence it has caused. Don't fight yourself, because you're not the enemy. The drug is the enemy. Think of it as a parasite that you have finally managed to expel but that, as in horror films, is trying to reinvade you. If you allow it to do so, you've lost. Hold yourself sacred; don't allow the enemy in, because once it has breached your defences not only will it be killing you but it will convince you that it is doing so for your own good.

We have now answered these questions:

* Is my smoking my own fault?
  No. You probably started because other people smoked and you knew no better. You became addicted within a week, after which you ceased to have control. No one has helped you to stop. You are a victim of the tobacco industry and other vested interests. You are responsible, but you are not to blame. Blaming yourself is pointless and will not help you to stop.
* How will I know when I've failed to stop?
  This seems like a silly question, but it isn't. You have only failed when you stop trying.
* How will I know when I've succeeded?
  This seems like an even sillier question. If you think your only target is never to smoke again, you will fail. Instead set a target that you can achieve, like not smoking for the next hour, day, week, month or year. Then you can succeed, because you will have set a target that *you* can achieve. Never accept other people's targets.
* What is the point of cutting down?

If you can't stop smoking, could you at least cut down? If you can, you will prove that you can achieve something. You will be a success, because you will have set a target and reached it. Having done that, when you are ready you can set a target of stopping and reach that target. Once again, learn to succeed by setting targets you can reach.

* Why can't I stop thinking about cigarettes when I stop smoking?

  Because you are addicted and psychologically dependent. The problem will not go away on its own, as you have discovered, but you will overcome it if you follow the programme in this book meticulously.

* Does stress make me smoke?

  When you are stressed, relieving low-level craving for nicotine will be interpreted by your brain as stress relief. So now, your response to stress is to smoke. There is in fact almost no connection, as you will discover when you deal with stress without smoking. It only works, though, if you take stress management seriously and alter your stress response *before* you attempt to stop smoking. Trying to deal with withdrawal symptoms *and* stress together will be much harder.

11

The After-Shock

WHAT IS IT GOING TO FEEL LIKE AS AN EX-SMOKER? WILL IT FEEL SO BAD THAT YOU'LL WANT TO SMOKE AGAIN?

Some of the questions answered in this chapter:

* If the addiction is finished in a few days, why do I still feel ill weeks later?
* Why do I suddenly find myself desperate to smoke weeks after I thought all craving had gone?

How you will feel after stopping – physically

Just imagine you have been ill for thirty years, and no one could find a cure for your disease. Then suddenly a cure is found, and you go into hospital for the treatment. Afterwards, the doctor comes to your bed and tells that you the treatment has been completely successful and you can go home. Naturally, they say, you will need to spend some time convalescing; you will be tired for a few weeks, and there will be aches and pains as your body recovers from thirty years of illness. That's what you would expect, isn't it?

Why is it, then, that patients who come to our clinics after smoking for thirty years are so surprised when they don't feel as fit as a flea the day after they stop?

The chemical punishment

Each time you smoke a cigarette, these are some of the biologically active agents you are consuming:

Carbon monoxide, nicotine, acetaldehyde, acetone, NOx, formic acid, hydrogen cyanide, catechol, ammonia, benzene, acrolein, acrylonitrile, phenol, formaldehyde, carbazole, 2-nitropropane, N'-nitrosonornicotine, 4-(methylnitrosamino)-1-(3-pyridil)-1-butanone, N'-nitrosoanabasine, N-nitrosodiethanolamine, N-nitrosopyrrolidine, N-nitrosodimethylamine, N-nitrosomethylethylamine, N-nitrosodiethylamine, N-nitrosodi-n-propylamine, N-nitrosodi-n-butylamine, N-nitrosopiperidine, hydrazine, urethane, vinyl chloride, benzanthracine, benzopyrene, 5-methylcrysene, dibenzacridine, 2-napthylamine, 4-aminobiphenyl, 2-toluidine, polonium-210.

Frightening, isn't it? And hardly surprising that it is going to take some time to recover. To put these ingredients in perspective, here is a list of the compounds you have been consuming, under their major groupings, with the number of individual compounds in brackets:

Amines, imides, lactones (240), carboxylic acids, anhydrides (240), lactones (150), esters (475), aldehydes (110), ketones (520), alcohols (380), phenols (285), amines (200), N-nitrosamines (22), N-heterocyclics (920), hydrocarbons (755), nitriles (105), carbohydrates (45), ethers (310).

This brings the total number of compounds you have been consuming to 4,865. Multiply that by the number of times you smoked each day, and you get some idea of your daily consumption of substances too awful even for E-numbers. Are you sure you enjoy smoking?

The effect on your body

If you have smoked for any length of time you will have damaged your body, particularly your lungs. It is not possible for the human body to inhale thousands of chemicals in a base of burning tar and not suffer. We are capable of taking a lot of punishment, but that is too much.

So the first thing to assume is that you have damaged your body by smoking. This applies even if you are unaware of it, on account of the body's wonderful ability to overcome much of the abuse to which we subject it. The amount of damage will depend not just on the type of tobacco you have smoked, how many you have smoked each day and for how many years, but also on your own strength – your body's ability to protect itself from what you do to it.

Diet is a good example of use and abuse. Much of the food consumed in the West does more harm than good, and yet many people seem to do quite well on it. This raises doubts in some people's minds about the importance of good diet – perhaps we really can eat any old junk. The human body does indeed possess the ability to survive on far less than the optimum diet, but your health would be very different if you ate a better diet. You might seem fine, but that doesn't mean you wouldn't be better on better food.

We in the West have become accustomed to compromising on our health. Time and time again we hear patients, and even doctors, treat ill health as an inevitable consequence of living. It is not. Almost everyone could enjoy better health and greater vigour than they currently do. We have lost the ability to distinguish between good health and indifferent health.

So, if you don't actually suffer from a smoking-related disease, such as emphysema, bronchitis or heart trouble, you might believe you have escaped completely. You haven't. You might not be aware of it while you are smoking; but you might very well become aware of it once you have stopped. We have seen that withdrawal symptoms are short-lived – a few days perhaps. And we have also seen that psychological withdrawal is long-term, sometimes lasting for years, but gradually diminishing. There is a third kind of withdrawal, though, that has nothing to do with addiction or dependence.

If you have smoked for, say, thirty years, your body is going to take time to adjust, as explained above. Just imagine its reaction to no longer getting its intake of twenty or thirty cigarettes a day, which previously represented a very significant proportion of your diet. Indeed many heavy smokers will, over the years, have replaced with tobacco a large amount of the food they used to eat. Imagine you had emigrated to another part of the world, where the food was nothing whatever like the food you are used to. You might have an upset stomach for a while until you adjusted. When you stop smoking that too represents a major change in your diet, so you should expect to feel unwell.

Another major change will take place in your lungs. If you fill them up with poisonous gases twenty or thirty times a day for thirty years, it is hardly surprising if they notice the difference when you stop doing so. The shock, however, is short-lived; within days your lungs will start to function better.

While you have been smoking you have been laying down tar in your lungs which stayed there simply because you kept putting more on top of it. Your lungs have never had the chance to fight back. But as soon as you stop smoking they can do just that. The result for many ex-smokers is coughs, colds, sore throats and a host of other infections which they never used to get. These infections are often interpreted by the new non-smoker as a problem. They might be problematic in that they are undesirable, but that doesn't mean they are going to cause a problem to your stop-smoking programme. People going through this process feel a great temptation to start smoking again, reasoning that smoking will stop them feeling ill – and they are right.

If a few weeks of convalescence is too high a price to pay for ending your smoking, don't bother. This convalescence period is inevitable, whether you stop smoking now or in five or ten years' time. No one has yet conducted any research to discover how many people go back to smoking because they mistake this convalescence for withdrawal symptoms, but we believe it is likely to be very high. Unfortunately, many new non-smokers go to their GP at this stage and complain about feeling unwell, and because GPs are not usually trained in addiction management or smoking cessation they are often unable to help. This is a major factor in making people take up smoking again. If more GPs understood this mechanism, they would be able to help people at this critical stage. It is particularly sad that these people will already have overcome the worst part – the addiction – and go back to smoking for what is really such a minor reason.

Withdrawal symptoms or convalescence?

So do expect to feel unwell after the first two or three days as an ex-smoker, and don't misidentify the way you feel as withdrawal symptoms. There is a simple test you can use to differentiate the two.

Withdrawal, for almost all smokers, will take place within hours of the last cigarette, or within a day or two in exceptional cases. People who come to our clinics don't go through this phase because we give them the neutrogen, so our Helpline staff know for certain at what point convalescence starts since there are no withdrawal symp-

123

toms to start with. But you will be dealing with the addiction phase on your own, so it is important that you make a written record of your withdrawal symptoms (for example, mood changes, sleeplessness and headaches).

If after two to four days these symptoms change, make another note. This change will probably represent the *progression from withdrawal to convalescence*. This is real progress. Whatever the new symptoms, they will inevitably diminish in time, possibly over a week or two.

Conversely, you will know when *convalescence* starts because it will be quite different from your withdrawal symptoms. As a rough guide, withdrawal will last a few days, but certainly less than a week.

There is a way you can be sure that this phase is not withdrawal. Always remember what withdrawal means – it is the symptoms you get when you are unable to satisfy a physical craving for your drug. If you are feeling rough, but you can honestly say that you don't have a strong craving to smoke, then this is not withdrawal but convalescence, and you are on the way to succeeding. Convalescence is often experienced as a problem, but don't look at it in that way: it a sign that you are coming through.

Many smokers experience a very nasty taste in the mouth when they stop, and often interpret this as a withdrawal symptom. It is not. The mouth is a primary escape route for the toxin-impregnated tar from your lungs, and this, unsurprisingly, doesn't taste nice. Better out than in. (One of our patients complained that the drops we gave her made her teeth go yellow. It wasn't the drops – the colour was coming from her own lungs.)

How you will feel after stopping – emotionally

We find that our patients go through quite a clear pattern of emotions, typically:

Before the treatment	Doubt about their motivation
	Doubt about our ability to help them
	Fear of failure
After the treatment	Doubt about their motivation
	Fear of success
Longer term	Doubt about their motivation
	Anger at us for stopping them smoking
	Resentment at the loss of pleasure

Although you will be stopping smoking on your own, you are likely to go through a very similar pattern. You will notice that the underlying emotion is always doubt about motivation. This is because so many people try to stop smoking for the wrong reason – because the world is telling them they should not or must not smoke. Even if the main reason is health, they don't stop because they really want to stop (which, given their addiction, is exactly what we should expect).

As you go through the withdrawal phase, the addiction will be challenging your motivation. As you go through the dependence phase, your dependence will be challenging your motivation. At all times, your motivation will be in doubt. You will be vulnerable. No matter what difficulties there are with stopping smoking, if people were totally motivated they would be able to overcome them. That you have not been able to overcome them proves that your motivation was insufficient.

Those in positions of authority over the nation's health try to convince us that we will stop smoking if we are motivated enough. What does 'enough' mean? Enough to overcome the terrible withdrawal symptoms that some smokers have? Enough to overcome the fear of never smoking again? Enough to overcome perhaps forty years of learned behaviour (habit)? In our clinics we consistently find that there is only one real way to give smokers good motivation – by making it easy for them to stop.

When you tried to stop smoking before, you presumably weren't sufficiently motivated (or you would have succeeded). If you succeeded before, but started smoking again, you simply had enough motivation to stop but not enough to stay stopped. We often find a backlash against stopping after two to four weeks of success: our patients suddenly wonder why they bothered in the first place. All of this raises questions about people's real reasons for wanting to stop. Before they stop, they are comfortably addicted to a drug that they believe gives them pleasure, that helps them to stay calm in times of stress, that they can enjoy with their friends. During the backlash phase they might well remember these things, and the memory seriously challenges their motivation. This, as you will realize, is what we have been calling psychological dependence. Understanding it will help you to overcome it, and in time it will get easier.

This backlash causes a lot of people to go back to smoking who otherwise were doing very well. Recognize that this is your dependence challenging you, and at this stage read Chapter 13.

No regrets?

After you have stopped, you will probably look at people smoking and envy them. They can do what you are no longer allowed to do. Well, you *are* allowed to do it. No one has stopped you except yourself. You decided to stop, for your own reasons, so why would you be jealous of people who are still smoking? Or, to put it another way, why would you regret what you have done? That you might regret it is not actually surprising, because you were not totally convinced you wanted to do it in the first place.

Addicts don't want to lose their addiction – that's what

addiction means. If you are pushed into stopping smoking (through health worries and so on) you are going to be in conflict before you even start – you need to stop, but you would prefer to continue. Always remember that wanting to continue is not quite 'real', though. After all, non-smokers don't want to start, so why would you want to continue? It's unlikely that, among the millions of people in Britain who have never smoked, you would find even one who wants to smoke and regrets not being able to. Why should this be? It's because there's no reason to smoke. Unless, of course, you are addicted, in which case you have no choice.

So what you regret is not being a non-smoker, but being an ex-smoker. People who have never smoked simply do not regret being non-smokers (which you must admit would be ridiculous). People who used to smoke often regret, at least for a while, being ex-smokers. It's possible that non-smokers don't know what they are missing, but it's more likely that ex-smokers are missing something. Let's look at what you might miss once you've stopped.

Your pleasure
We looked at this idea in Chapter 8. The enjoyment you used to get was mainly the result of continually satisfying low-level cravings for nicotine, even if you were not conscious of them. However, most ex-smokers miss what they think of as the pleasure of smoking, and you might not want to be told that the pleasure was all in your mind – after all, that's where you feel all pleasures, isn't it?

In a way, yes. But, if the pleasure is actually relief from 'displeasure' (low-level craving), because it's really only a fix of your drug, then the pleasure is not a real one, and sooner or later you will have to come to terms with this fact. The pleasure of smoking is largely the pleasure of drug addiction, which is always false.

So what you have to do every time you find yourself

pining for the lost enjoyment is read this section over and over again, until you believe it.

Your friend

Many patients, when they first come to our clinics, talk of cigarettes as being some kind of friend they are going to miss. We could state the obvious – with a friend that is going to shorten your life, who needs enemies? – but we won't. Again, this is the addiction talking. Tobacco is only a friend in as much as you are dependent on it, like you might be with a true friend. The dependence is real, but that doesn't make tobacco a true friend.

Nevertheless, it is going to take time for you to accept all this. Meanwhile, it is quite all right to mourn the loss of your 'friend'. It is difficult to know how to advise patients in this respect, because everyone is different. Whilst we find it is helpful for patients to have a period of mourning, some are so psychologically dependent that they cannot cope with anything but complete rejection at the point of stopping smoking. The best advice is: don't be afraid to feel sorry for yourself, and sorry for the loss. This might be healthier than pretending to be glad you have stopped, when really you are feeling bereft.

Your crutch

When you smoke your last cigarette, your overwhelming feeling is likely to be fear – of the unknown. How are you going to manage without cigarettes?

Probably like everyone else. At this point you are highly dependent on tobacco, and this dependence takes time to overcome. But no one remains dependent on a drug they haven't had for years. So you can be quite sure that the time will come when you will be managing very well without tobacco. The only question is, not how will you manage, but how long will it be before you can manage?

Some ex-smokers say they will always feel a little sad about stopping. This doesn't mean they are still dependent. It means they used to be dependent, and addicted, and they will pay a small price for that for the rest of their lives. But that doesn't matter, and it is certainly no reason to start smoking again.

We have now answered these questions:

* If the addiction is finished in a few days, why do I still feel ill weeks later?

    Withdrawal symptoms make you feel ill, but they stop in a few days. The next phase is convalescence, which is not withdrawal at all. It is the healing process that your body goes through after years of drug abuse. If you remember not to confuse these two phases you won't make the mistake of thinking you are still addicted weeks later.

* Why do I suddenly find myself desperate to smoke weeks after I thought all craving had gone?

    It is a common mistake to think that this is still withdrawal, but it can't be. Once your withdrawal symptoms have gone, they don't come back. This happens *because* the addiction has gone. You are succeeding, and your subconscious is fighting this success; this is the psychological dependence. Don't fight your own success.

12

If That's Your Attitude

CHANGE IT NOW, BEFORE YOU START.

At the moment, assuming you are seriously contemplating trying to stop smoking, you have a list of problems. For example:

* How will you cope with stress without cigarettes?
* How will you overcome the terrible craving?
* How will you avoid being bad-tempered?
* How will you cope with changing your habits?
* How will you still enjoy socializing if you can't smoke?
* How will you control your weight?
* How will you fill your more boring days?
* What will you do with your hands?
* What will you do if you fail?

You can probably think of some more yourself.

And while you are doing a spot of thinking, consider something else too. If you had never smoked in your life, would you now be faced with these problems? No. So the problems aren't caused by not smoking, but by *stopping* smoking. And if they are problems that non-smokers don't have, it is clear that you won't have them either once you have stopped.

For all of these problems this book contains both a practical and an emotional answer. Stop believing that being a non-smoker is going to make life worse, or harder, or less enjoyable. It is only addicts who believe their drug actually improves their lives.

Having started to undo the myth of life being better for smokers, start to look at how life might be better for non-smokers:

* They have better health
* They will live longer
* They don't smell of stale cigarettes
* Like credit cards, they are accepted everywhere
* They are richer
* They don't have stained hands
* They don't have to worry about their drug supply
* They don't feel guilty
* And they are free.

When we ask our patients what they feel is the greatest benefit once they have stopped smoking, the most frequent answer is that they are free – by which they mean free of the addiction and free of the dependence. When they have stopped smoking, they come to realize that their fears were caused by their addiction, and that their belief in the pleasure was caused by the addiction as well. If you live in a country run by a totalitarian dictatorship it is easy to believe it is a benevolent one because it tells you so. In the case of smoking, the dictatorship of tobacco has convinced you of its benevolence.

The freedom to smoke

Smokers believe they have to protect their freedom to smoke, often where and when they want. But this is a terrible, tragic joke.

Smokers are not free. If they were free, why would they fear stopping? If they were free, they would be able to do what they want – but they cannot. It is non-smokers who are free. A non-smoker is free to make a choice – to smoke or not to smoke, as he or she pleases. You, a smoker, do not have that choice because you have been unable to stop smoking (which is why you are reading this book). So stop telling yourself you are free to smoke. You have been had. The tobacco companies insist that you have the right to smoke. What they mean is they have the right to sell you a drug that is going to shorten your life. Whenever you are tempted to believe in the myth of freedom, remember that the freedom the tobacco companies are talking about is the freedom for them to profit from your addiction.

If you are addicted to anything you are a slave, and slaves are not free. Become a non-smoker, because non-smokers have a choice. *Then* you will be free.

Problems, problems

Not only do non-smokers not have the problems you do, but they also have fewer health and money worries and less guilt. Despite this, you are the one who is worried. Smoking has given you these problems, and it is quite logical that stopping smoking will remove them (notwithstanding any temporary difficulty while you are in the process of becoming a non-smoker). But it is not usually these temporary problems that worry would-be ex-smokers.

For example, you may be genuinely worried about what you will do with your hands when you stop smoking. This problem is caused at first by low-level cravings for nicotine, and afterwards because people believe they are addicted – the psychological dependence. But you had no problem with your hands before you started smoking, so why should you afterwards? Only because the dependence takes some time to get over. The problem exists because you have smoked, not because you have stopped.

Perhaps you worry about how you are going to fill your days without cigarettes, particularly if you have an unexciting job. If this describes you, ask your non-smoking colleagues how they cope. It is unlikely that you cope any better than they do simply because you smoke, even though it is common for people in boring jobs to pace themselves with cigarettes. And you do have a choice: to help, if you really want to, you can use a drug that kills three hundred users a day.

Many would-be ex-smokers worry about putting on weight if they stop smoking. It takes a weight gain of about three and a half stone to give you the same health risk as smoking twenty cigarettes a day, so what are you worrying about? If you are concerned about the health risks of getting overweight, by all means use a drug that gives people heart disease to keep your weight down. If you are worried about your looks, how do you think you look walking round with a fag hanging out of your mouth and smelling like an old ashtray?

In reality non-smokers are no heavier than smokers. What causes you to put on weight is the act of stopping, which may cause you temporarily to overeat because you substitute food for cigarettes. In other words, if you had never smoked the problem would very probably not exist. If the act of stopping smoking might cause you to put on weight, then do it in such a way that it does not – deal with the addiction properly. And if you do put weight on, you can lose it again. Losing weight is always going to be easier than stopping smoking, so do get your priorities right.

To summarize, you can see that the problems you are currently faced with exist not because you are going to be a non-smoker, but because you have been a smoker. Realize that these problems cannot last for ever, and that they will be gone once you are a happy non-smoker. At the moment you are causing your own problems, because of your fear. And why do you have this fear?

Because you are an addict, and all addicts are afraid of losing their drug. Once you have overcome the addiction you will gain control over your psychological dependence, and with that control your fear will disappear.

Pressures from outside

Some years ago, the NHA was asked by an insurance company to help staff in their computer department to stop smoking. After the first batch went through the clinic we never heard from them again, although the programme involves constant telephone monitoring of patients. So when the second batch attended, we asked them what had happened to the first lot. Apparently the company's no-smoking policy had been handled so badly that all the staff had volunteered for treatment, but agreed among themselves that they would not actually use the neutrogen and would not stop smoking. It seemed to them a good way of getting back at the company. How sad it is that they were prepared to shorten their lives to spite their employer. It is never worth smoking to spite others. It really is cutting off your nose to spite your face.

If your employer is imposing a ban on smoking in the workplace, it is probably not for your benefit. It is for the benefit of the non-smokers, and ultimately of the employer who doesn't don't want to be faced with future lawsuits for illness caused by passive smoking.

You might resent this intrusion, although a number of smokers do say they wish smoking were outlawed because it is the only way they are ever going to stop. We agree: tobacco products should be sold in a much more controlled way, particularly to prohibit their sale to children. But the government has shown that economic issues outweigh the health of the nation, and as long as the country is being run as a business, instead of a place fit for people to live in, this will continue to be so.

Many smokers tell us they resent the government's attitude, and also that of doctors who preach but don't help. In the case of doctors, it is probably more a case of inability to help than unwillingness. Doctors can only give their patients what the system, and their training, gives them. The NHA has tried hard to interest GPs in being trained to neutralize tobacco addiction, but without success. This is not their fault; without financial backing, we have not had the resources to get the message across. (That is one of the reasons for writing this book; the proceeds will help us to help GPs provide neutralization under the National Health Service.)

Much of the pressure being put on smokers is well-meaning but inept. If you feel pressured by your employer, your family and friends, the media, your GP or society generally, try to ignore it. It is highly unlikely that these people understand your problems, but resist the temptation to assert your freedom to smoke because of them. You are the only one who will suffer.

Pity the children

Many smokers say they want to stop for their children's sake. If this is the motivation you need, fine. You might well wish you had never started to smoke as a child; if you did, it was probably because you saw adults smoke. As a society we are still teaching children to smoke. The next time you are in a tobacconist's/sweet shop look how the sweets are arranged: it is impossible for children not to see the cigarettes displayed directly behind them. The message is clear: when you are small you buy sweets, and when you grow up you buy the things displayed higher up – cigarettes. As long as cigarettes are sold in sweetshops and supermarkets we are wasting our time telling children they shouldn't smoke, because they simply won't believe us.

If you have teenage children, you may have experienced an interesting phenomenon. Schoolchildren are often violently opposed to smoking – until they come under peer pressure. At the NHA we have seen an astonishing transformation when this happens; young people simply cannot resist the pressure. Nothing you can say is going to help, because *you* smoke. The only way you can contribute to their survival in this jungle is not to lecture them, but to make sure they see what a hell of a time you have trying to stop smoking. Let them share in the misery, and let them be absolutely clear on your attitude – that you wish you had never started, that you hate the smell on your body, on your clothes and in your home, that you resent wasting all that money, that the tobacco companies are using you to make profit, and that you smoke not because you enjoy it but because you have no choice.

Of course, you might not believe all these things. However, if you can convince your children you might convince yourself.

Nothing comes easy

Every smoker who wants to stop knows that he or she will have to work at it. Why is it, then, that they are so often surprised when it turns out to be really hard work?

The answer is that most smokers live on platitudes. 'Smoking is bad for me', 'You have to want to stop if you are going to succeed', and so on. But recognizing that it is going to require an effort is not usually enough. Just take a little time to think through the changes you are going to be making:

* You are on a drug which is as addictive as heroin.
* You are habituated to an activity which you have done more than anything else in your life (see p 42).
* You have probably failed to stop before and are afraid of failing again.
* You are afraid of a life without cigarettes.

All of this is going to have to be changed. It can certainly be done, because hundreds, if not thousands, of people stop smoking every day. You need knowledge, which you are getting from this book; you need support, which is also available (see pg 209 for details of the NHA Helpline); you need determination, and only time will tell if you have enough. What you also need, as with any job this important, is a commitment to make the effort and find the time.

Do start thinking of stopping smoking as a positive rather than a negative activity. Not smoking is negative – you are trying *not* to do something. But becoming a non-smoker is positive – you are trying to *be* something. Stopping smoking means losing something. Becoming a non-smoker means gaining something.

Your stop-smoking programme is a major event in your life. Devote to it the time and thought you would give to any other big project. View it in the same light as finding a new job, moving house or starting a new relationship – all things which you would expect to occupy a great deal of your time, thoughts and energy. This book, like all the help we give to patients, involves *self*-help; our success is due to our policy of giving people the knowledge and support to enable them to help themselves.

The three programmes that follow in Part Two, Preparation, Cessation and Maintenance, are tried and tested, and they really work. But they only work if they are tackled systematically and conscientiously. Please put time and effort into them, because we want you to succeed.

Part Two

Stopping

13

Becoming a Non-Smoker

PLANNING YOUR OWN INDIVIDUAL PROGRAMME

If you have ever tried to stop smoking before, with the help of a book, a video or a support group, the process will have involved:

* First: plan your programme.
* Second: stop smoking.
* Third: solve the problems that arise.

This sounds fine until you take it apart. If you could solve the problems that arise from stopping smoking, you wouldn't need to make any plans and you would probably have stopped smoking long ago.

We are going to suggest a very different approach. You know you need a different approach, because you have failed previous attempts (so they didn't suit you), or you have never tried (you didn't find a way that suited you), or you stopped smoking but went back to it (you found a way that suited you, but it wasn't the answer you wanted because otherwise you would try it again).

Having read this far, you should have a much better understanding of your smoking problem than you had before. You might think that, with this knowledge, you can go on to stop smoking. Well, almost. Don't use this knowledge simply to repeat your previous mistakes. You have already come this far with us, so please bear with us a little longer – with the help of our patients we have amassed a mountain of knowledge and experience, which means we still know things you don't and which we want to share with you.

Start at the end

If every conventional stop-smoking scheme leaves you with problems that you can't resolve (so you fail), doesn't it make a lot of sense to solve the problems before you actually start the programme? It's always easier to pre-empt a problem rather than solve it when you are in the middle of it. Right now, you are concentrating rationally on how to stop smoking. You might not be so rational when you haven't had a cigarette for three days.

Many books on stopping smoking tell you to plan your attempt. This if all very well if you know what to plan, but the books tend to be very thin on real, hard information. So before you plan the actual attempt, look at the likely problems.

Imagine an attempt on Mount Everest were being planned. It would not include the purchase of equipment until the climbers knew *what* equipment they might need, and this would mean assessing the terrain, the weather, their skills and many other factors. Similarly, you don't know what 'equipment' you are going to need to stop smoking until you have assessed your own unique problems. In other words, don't try to overcome those problems until you have worked out exactly what they are. This may sound terribly obvious – but if it is, why do so many people buy products over the chemist's counter which are supposed to stop them smoking, but which are identical for all the millions of smokers who buy them? If every smoker were identical, and the chemist's cure worked for just one smoker, it would work for every smoker. That

144

is does not is proof that each smoker has a special mix of problems that have to be resolved.

You already know the problems

You cannot have read this far without learning what the problems are. We have already seen that many would-be ex-smokers are unable to rationalize and express their inability to succeed. You might have been one of them. By now you should be able to express your problems clearly.

Exercise

At this point write down your reasons for not being able to stop smoking or for going back to smoking once you have stopped. Here's a typical list. It might not have looked like this before you read this book, but it is now based on a better understanding of the actual issues:

* Addiction (e.g. craving/irritability and other symptoms)
* Psychological dependence (e.g. fear of failing/fear of succeeding)
* Stress (e.g. a disaster would make you smoke)
* Social (e.g. your friends/partner/family smoke)
* Habit (e.g. what will you do after meals?)
* Enjoyment (e.g. you are going to miss smoking sometimes)
* Motivation (e.g. why do you want to stop anyway?)
* Anything else (e.g. don't know what to do with your hands)

This list, being a selective sample only, is not exhaustive. Yours will be, so take your time, be thorough, and above all be absolutely honest.

Now, if you were going through a conventional attempt to stop smoking, you would probably have all these issues to deal with at once. Instead of doing that you going to deal with them separately, and you are going to resolve them *before* actually stopping smoking.

It might have occurred to you that this is some kind of trick – that if you could resolve these problems of course you could stop smoking. It is not a trick – or, at least, it is only a trick in the sense that the clever part is to resolve the problems consecutively and in the right order. For example, if you have a fear of succeeding, it is going to be difficult to overcome this a week after you had your last cigarette – when you will be in the middle of succeeding! Perhaps you have a fear of failing instead. This could be very tricky if you are suffering withdrawal symptoms such as irritability. And if you have a fear of failing at the same time as a fear of succeeding (which is not uncommon), at the same time as withdrawal symptoms – and your worried friends are offering you cigarettes 'to calm you down', the cat has just been sick on the bed, and your hands feel utterly desperate for something to hold – which of these problems are you going to solve first? Why don't you have a cigarette while you figure it out?

So which one do you solve first?

You decide. It makes a lot of sense, though, to start with the problem that has the *least* to do with smoking. By doing it this way, smoking itself is not the issue. And, from long experience with patients, we know that this is likely to be stress. Stress has nothing whatever to do with smoking; both smokers and non-smokers suffer stress.

Let's go through our list of a typical smoker's problems and suggest how they could be tackled, and in which order. A lot of it will apply directly to you. If it is not exactly the way you would do it, go through the exercise and then write out your own programme based on it.

Part 1: dealing with stress

For this stage you need Chapter 9. Taking control of your own life has nothing to do with giving up smoking. It is about removing a major obstacle so you can finally do what you want, which is to stop smoking. Decide right now what you are going to do about stress. Do not, however, be put off your stop-smoking programme because this task seems too daunting. Just set yourself a target date by which you should achieve *something*. So we are not suggesting that you simply remove all the stress in your life so that you can stop smoking (some smokers say they need a little stress to keep them going. This is a misunderstanding; by 'stress' we always mean excessive stress).

There are of course many different ideas on dealing with stress, so please do reread Chapter 9. For this exercise, let's look at your options.

Altering your stress response

* You could go to yoga classes.
* You could go to some other kind of relaxation classes.
* You could study the subject seriously from books.
* You could take a homoeopathic remedy.
* You could take regular exercise.
* You could switch drugs – like having a small drink each day (one glass of red wine a day is more likely to be helpful than harmful, and will not make you an alcohol addict. But low-level smoking, say five a day, will turn you into an addict, will lead to much higher consumption, and will shorten your life).

Reducing stressors

You could decrease your stress load as described in Chapter 9. This would prevent you becoming overloaded, and going back to tobacco in an attempt to cope with that overload.

And remember, there is something very positive you can

do about the cigarettes themselves. You can smoke less. Not enough to challenge your addiction, not enough to put you under stress, not enough to make you afraid of giving up, not enough to spoil the 'enjoyment' of smoking. But enough to get started, because this will make you feel good.

Part One, unless you are one of the rare people for whom stress is not a problem, is unlikely to last less than several weeks, and could go on for months. When you are feeling better about the control you are taking over your life, and you have cut down your consumption of tobacco a little, you are ready for stage two.

But one last word before you move forward. All the time you are in Part One, remember one vital fact. No matter what stress you come under in future, if you smoke one cigarette to cope with it you could become readdicted and spend the rest of your life smoking. Ask yourself, every day, if this is a price you are prepared to pay for a moment's relief from the problem.

Part 2: dealing with the habit

For this stage you need Chapters 5, 6 and 8. We have seen that most smokers feel they cannot stop because of the habit, but that habit is very much in your control. This part is about working out how to take control over your habits and deliberately alter them.

Doing so will put you in a much stronger position when you come to stop smoking, and will also demonstrate that you really can control what you do. Since stopping smoking is so much about self-control, now is the time to train yourself to exercise it.

Our patients find it quite exciting when they realize they can change their smoking habit. If you do it because you have stopped smoking (so you have no choice) it's very hard. But if you do it without stopping smoking it becomes a pleasure. And we are of course talking about changing habits, not about breaking them. The purpose of this particular exercise is not to stop you smoking but to enable you to smoke at different times; in other words, to teach yourself to control when you smoke. If you can do this, you will learn that you can decide, in any given situation, whether you smoke or not.

A warning, though: don't try to go without the first one of the day during this or any other preliminary stage. This is needed to maintain your addiction, and doing without it will put yourself under pressure.

The best way to learn to change your habits is to do it in a way that does not hurt you or put pressure on you. You probably smoke at certain times – like after meals, when you get in the car, and so on. The way to change this pattern is to deliberately not smoke at those particular times, but to smoke at any other time. For example, in week one you might decide not to smoke after meals, in week two you might decide not to smoke when you are on the telephone either. In week three, you might decide not to smoke when you get in the car, but (and this suggestion might surprise you) to go back to smoking after meals. And in week four, stop the after-meals cigarette again.

What you are doing here is not just changing your habits, but learning the truth about habit – that you can change it at will. You can smoke or not smoke after lunch. And you have this control because you are not putting yourself under pressure by trying to stop at the same time.

You cut down the number of cigarettes you smoke in Part One, and you will cut down even further in Part Two. While you are changing habits you should find your consumption comes down naturally.

The habit-changing stage will only last a few weeks if you are good at it, but take a couple of months if you feel more comfortable with it. In fact, the longer you take, the more completely in control you are likely to be.

Our habits do not control us; they only appear to do so because we have no great need to control them. The reason you have been unable to control your smoking so far has nothing to do with habit. You are addicted and psychologically dependent (to be dealt with next), which means you will smoke because you have to. This makes you habituated, but habit does not make you need to smoke. Always remember this.

Part 3: dealing with psychological dependence

For this stage you need Chapters 3 and 6. We are now getting into the major issues – ones which can't necessarily be completely resolved before you stop smoking.

First reread the relevant chapters so that you understand better what dependence is and why it stops you stopping. Then you will be able to put into practice what you have learnt – though not until immediately after you actually stop smoking.

At this point you must get down on paper your own understanding of your dependence, which doesn't include your addiction or the habit. Let's look at some likely dependence problems and some possible answers:

Fear of failure

When you take your driving test, fear of failure is a major factor. It is perhaps not until you have failed it once or twice that you have the confidence to succeed. Read through Chapter 10 again, particularly the section about not allowing yourself the luxury of failure. Forget any past failures. Tackle the problems as we prescribe, resolve them, and you will have the confidence to stop smoking.

Fear of success

About half the patients in our clinics fear never smoking again. The reason is that they believe they have to succeed totally and immediately. In their most rational moments they admit that they actually quite look forward to a life free from smoking, so what makes them afraid of succeeding is the process of stopping.

The only people who are afraid of never smoking again are smokers – it doesn't affect non-smokers or ex-smokers. So stop smoking and you will be able to face the future as an ex-smoker. The secret here is to face only one day at a time. Twenty-four hours after you had your last cigarette the future will look less frightening. After a week you will even start to look forward to the future. So follow this golden rule: forget the future, just take it one day at a time.

Belief that you need to smoke to cope with stress
For this one reread Chapter 9. The reason this association makes you psychologically dependent is fear: smokers tend to be afraid that smoking is the only way to handle stress. By following this programme properly you will start to tackle stress and discover that, whatever happens, you can find something better than smoking to deal with it.

And remember, non-smokers manage every bit as well as smokers. When you are an ex-smoker you will still cope with your life, but as a bonus you will not have the stress that smoking imposes on you now – like health worries, cost and guilt.

Belief that you will always be addicted
Addiction is self-perpetuating because your body is trying to maintain its adaptation to a poison – in this case nicotine. Once the addiction is broken, which takes only about a week without tobacco, what you are left with is only the psychological dependence.

So don't confuse addiction and habit, or addiction and psychological dependence. Remember, the dependence is an irrational fear. Rationalizing what is happening to you will help you to overcome that fear.

Belief that the habit is impossible to break
The reason for this is brainwashing. As long as doctors and others who should know better persist in calling it a habit, smokers will believe the habit keeps them smoking. Smoking is a habit, true, but that is not the reason you cannot stop. You can change your habits, and if you are following this programme properly you will have already taken this project in hand. So we should at this point be preaching to the converted.

Uncertainty about whether you really want to stop
Ninety per cent of the smokers whom we see in our clinics confess they are unsure about their motivation. The other 10 per cent are kidding themselves, because any smoker who is 100 per cent motivated to stop will do so without spending money on medical treatment.

The biggest single reason why smokers are unsure whether they really want to stop, or that they have enough motivation to succeed, is that they simply don't believe they can. Time and time again we find that a patient's motivation changes dramatically after the first dose of the neutrogen, because this immediately stops the craving for nicotine. This in turn convinces them that they are in control – for the first time they can decide for themselves whether they want to smoke or not, and whether they want to stop or not.

We sincerely hope that by reading this book carefully you will come to believe you can succeed in becoming a nonsmoker. Having taken steps to control the stress in your life, and then having learnt to change your smoking patterns/ habits, should make you feel a lot more confident. And while you go through these stages, you should, if you follow our instructions, be smoking less than you used to. You will be making progress. In fact, since you won't have failed anything, you will be succeeding. Well done. Even now your motivation is almost certainly greater than it was when you started reading this book.

Worry that you will miss the enjoyment
The thought of missing the enjoyment of smoking will also reduce your motivation, so read Chapter 8 again. If smoking were so great, everyone would do it. That they do not means either it is not as good as you think it is, or it is but the price (in financial or health terms) is too high. That is not to say you won't miss smoking. Of course you will. But it is very important that you turn this round. You are going to learn to enjoy the freedom from smoking more than you enjoy smoking.

It won't seem like that now – but to an addict it never does. If you were to ask me, as an ex-smoker, whether I get more enjoyment from my life without smoking, I could only say Yes. If you want to get really basic, ask yourself which you would enjoy more, smoking or lung cancer. You might fret over losing your enjoyment at the moment, but it passes. Many ex-smokers still hanker after the smell of someone else's cigarette, but that is as far as it goes.

Fear of pressure from friends and relatives while you are trying to stop
This pressure can make life very difficult, but it can usually be dealt with satisfactorily. To start with, get your family and friends to read Chapter 18. This should persuade them to take the pressure off.

Many of our patients don't tell anyone they are joining our programme because they are afraid of this pressure. But some patients tell everyone, deliberately, because they actually want that pressure. So it can work either way, depending on the patient's own psychology.

Having got this far in your programme you should be feeling a lot stronger than when you started reading the book, so you might be ready to face up to your friends and ask them for their support. And having come this far you are ready to start your preparations for becoming a non-smoker. You are going to be working through three separate programmes.

The three phases of stopping smoking

In this book, as you already know, we take you through three programmes – Preparation, Cessation and Maintenance. In the Preparation Programme you deal with the issues that caused you to fail before, except the addiction itself. In the Cessation Programme you experiment with mild withdrawal symptoms, to remove the fear, then you stop smoking. Having dealt with the psychological issues first, this is going to be like never before. Finally, in the Maintenance Programme you cover the period immediately after stopping, and then the long term.

If you are tempted to work through the these programmes in the wrong order you will be wasting your time, which is, sadly just what you have done with your previous failed attempts. Have patience; enjoy your programmes. You will know when you are ready to stop smoking.

But whatever method you use to stop, you will go through three phases.

Phase 1 – withdrawal
Starts: day one. Ends: one week later
In this phase you have to overcome your physical addiction – the chemical changes in your brain which happen while you lose your adaptation to your drug. This phase is dealt with in the Cessation Programme.

Withdrawal from nicotine starts within hours of your last fix, and lasts up to a week, but no longer.

Phase 2 – convalescence
Starts: within days. Ends: within weeks
This is the phase in which you can certainly feel ill, but it is separate from withdrawal symptoms. Unfortunately it tends to occur at the same time as withdrawal, which is why so many people think they are still withdrawing when they are in their second week.

Convalescence starts within hours (or days at the most) of stopping smoking, and can last several weeks – but this is very variable. Symptoms can range from hardly noticeable to severe.

Phase 3 – psychological dependence
Starts: long before you stop smoking. Ends: years after stopping
This includes everything else. These issues are dealt with in the Preparation Programme, but have to be controlled well into the Maintenance Programme.

Psychological dependence will start to be a problem even before you stop smoking, because of the fear and conflicts in making the decision to stop. It will continue for the rest of your life – but of course you don't have to let that be a problem.

14

The Preparation Programme

BREAK YOUR DEPENDENCE BEFORE YOU STOP SMOKING

You will now be well aware that you are going to tackle each issue separately, in the best order, before going on to the next problem. Then when the Preparation Programme has been completed to the best of your ability, you will be going on to the Cessation Programme. Being quite ready is your best guarantee of success.

Your target at the end of the Preparation Programme is to be ready to stop because you have dealt with the problems you would normally have *after* you stop smoking. By overcoming these problems first, the stopping part is going to be much less painful and the likelihood of success is very greatly increased.

Part 1 – stress

First read Chapter 9. All three stages are done at the same time.

Stage 1
Draw your stress barrel. Spend some days looking at absolutely every stressor. Only when this is complete should you start to analyse it. Which of your stressors are most easily dealt with? Remember, they will probably not seem important to you, but dealing with them will lower

the level in the barrel. This stage is likely to take at least a week.

Stage 2
Read through the section on breathing and establish a daily practice routine on waking, at your midday break, in the early evening and on going to bed. This means you are going to spend two minutes, four times a day, bringing your breathing under control. Throughout the day you are going to remember to think about your breathing, and correct it as necessary. At the end of each week you are going to review your progress chart. It will take at least four weeks to achieve some competence, and it will be several months before good breathing is making each day more relaxed.

Stage 3
You are going to investigate local yoga classes or other relaxation classes. Then you are going to join one. Our patients are often tempted to think that controlling stress is an optional part of the programme. It can be fatal to think that.

Timing
Dealing with stress is going to take about six weeks. Don't forget, you are not going to stop smoking during this period. You are going to bring your stress response under control, so that when you do finally stop you are going to be able to stay stopped.

Part 2 – habit

First read Chapter 5. Please note that when we say below that you should refrain from smoking for half an hour, this is for moderate smokers on up to twenty a day. Decreas-

this time to twenty minutes if you are on forty a day, and to just ten minutes if you smoke sixty.

This part of the programme is about learning to change your habits, so that eventually you can change them at will. Treat it as a game, because what you change them to is not important – you are not changing your habits because you have stopped smoking; you are changing them to prove that you are in control.

At no time during this part of the programme will you actually stop smoking. What you don't need at this stage is withdrawal symptoms.

Warning: although you will be reducing your smoking there is one cigarette which you must not leave out – the first smoke of the day. This is an important addiction cigarette and must be maintained, otherwise you will put yourself under pressure, which is the opposite of what you should be doing.

Stage 1

Write down a list of the times you normally expect to smoke. Even though you smoke throughout the day there will be certain cigarettes which are a kind of ritual, like after a meal, with a cup of coffee, on a long telephone call and so on. These are your target cigarettes which you are going to learn to manipulate, so that when you finally stop smoking they have been dealt with before they can pose a problem. This stage is completed on day one.

Stage 2

Pick one of the cigarettes on your list, for example the one after lunch. How long can you put off smoking after a meal - half an hour? If you have to smoke immediately *before* the meal, that's fine, because it won't interfere with what we are doing here.

For a week, you are not going to smoke for the half-hour after lunch. You will be under no stress whatever, because you can smoke at any other time. For the following week you are not going to smoke for half an hour after dinner either. So this stage takes a total of two weeks.

Stage 3
After two weeks of not smoking after lunch, and one of not smoking after dinner either, it is time to look at one of your other target cigarettes. Look, for example, at the one you smoke with a cup of coffee – not every cup but just one. Once a day you are going to drink a cup of coffee (or tea) without a cigarette. This is to prove to yourself that it is possible to drink without smoking.

After a week you are going to stop smoking with *all* your cups of coffee and tea. However, you are going to smoke at other times. This is not about stopping smoking, remember; it is about exercising control without being under pressure. All you need do is refrain from smoking for half an hour after starting to drink your cup of coffee.

Stage 4
You might not like it, but in this stage you are going to go backwards. So far you have lost some of your habit cigarettes, and you will be feeling that loss. It is important to prove to yourself that you are not losing but controlling.

So now you are going to reinstate one of your habits. For one week go back to smoking a cigarette immediately after lunch. At the end of the week, stop it again. Now go back to smoking after dinner. After one week, stop that as well.

So you see, you can change your smoking habits at will now. You are in control. Well done. This stage takes a total of two weeks.

Stage 5
During this stage you can play around with your habits a you like. From now on you don't smoke with a cup of tea o

160

coffee, or after meals, but what you can also do is stop any of the other target cigarettes.

Timing

The habit-changing part of your programme should be complete after about two months. At the end of this period you will not have stopped smoking – but never again will you be able to say that smoking is a habit you cannot control.

Part 3 – enjoyment

First read Chapter 8. This part of the programme is about changing your attitudes to smoking, and Chapter 8 explains the issues. What you have to do now is move from understanding them to believing them. The way you are going to do this is to experience pleasure that does not depend on smoking.

Warning: Once again don't try to cut out that first smoke of the day, your important addiction cigarette.

Stage 1

Choose a situation in which you normally particularly enjoy a cigarette. For our example we'll use a social setting in which you have a glass in one hand. Normally, when you are trying to stop smoking, this is a difficult time, because you are trying to overcome your desire to smoke at the same time as experiencing withdrawal symptoms, as well as the stress that goes with the thought that you will never be allowed to smoke again.

Well, you can smoke again, as soon as you get out of the pub. You are still a smoker, you just don't smoke in the pub. If you like you can even cut out only certain days. Let's say you normally go to the pub twice a week – just don't smoke on one of them. If you think your drink is less enjoyable because you aren't smoking you are fooling yourself. You don't have a cigarette on the go every minute you are in the pub, so a cigarette is not absolutely necessary. It is not the smoking you enjoy, but the ability to smoke. You *can* smoke – but not right then. Allow at least three weeks for this stage, because you might not like it at first.

Stage 2
This stage involves cutting out another occasion on which you particularly 'enjoy' a cigarette. What you are doing here is relearning the idea that going to the pub is enjoyable for its own sake. It must be, because non-smokers enjoy it.

Don't forget, you are still smoking. You can have a cigarette just before you get to the pub, and another as soon as you leave, but not while you are there. Now you are going to enjoy another social setting without smoking. Keep doing this for at least three weeks, because it will take time to get used to it.

Timing
Overall, expect to work on breaking the association between enjoyment and smoking over a period of at least six weeks.

Part 4 – consumption

First read Chapter 10. There is a common belief that the more cigarettes you smoke, the harder it will be to stop. But quantity is related to habit, enjoyment, stress and other psychological factors, and these things have nothing to do with stopping. Stopping means facing the addiction itself – getting past the Addiction Threshold. This part of the programme involves getting *down* to the Addiction Threshold, but not trying to get past it. That way you won't challenge your addiction, so you won't suffer any with drawal symptoms. You will become a very light smoker – the ideal position from which to stop smoking.

How much you reduce your smoking will of course depend on how many you smoke to start with.

Stage 1 (start here if you smoke sixty-plus)

If you currently smoke sixty a day or more, your task is to get down to forty a day. This is the easiest part, because most of the cigarettes you smoke are for the least important reasons – boredom, mindless habit, and because you have just never bothered to do anything about it. Since you have already gone through Parts 1, 2 and 3 of the Preparation Programme (stress, habit and enjoyment), it is likely that by now you have reduced your consumption quite a lot anyway.

You should allow at least one week for this stage. Having got down to forty, you will remain in this stage for a further two weeks. Don't go on to the next stage until you have stabilized on forty.

Stage 2 (start here if you smoke forty-plus)

You are now going to spend a week cutting down to twenty a day. Because you are not challenging your addiction, this requires only concentration and a reasonable level of determination. If you think you can't do it, how do you think you are going to stop smoking altogether? Twenty a day is typical of most British smokers, and most of them would say they are afraid to stop smoking – all you have to do is join them. Twenty a day is still four times as many as you need to satisfy your addiction. Once you have got to this level, you must remain on it for three weeks minimum. You can stay on it for longer if you want – the longer you stabilize on twenty the better.

You might be afraid of creeping up again. Why would you? Smoking twenty a day is easy. If you creep up again, it's because you can't be bothered even to exert a small degree of control. Remember, at this point stress, habit and other psychological factors shouldn't be an obstacle because you will have taken control. If they *are* a problem, you must go back a stage. Never push yourself further than you are ready to go. On the other hand, this is the time to start exercising self-discipline of a kind you might have thought you did not possess.

So now you are going to be a twenty-a-day smoker for a while. Take your time. Get used to it.

Stage 3. (start here if you smoke twenty-plus)
If you were a heavy smoker before, you are now an average smoker. If you are starting at this point, don't worry about the stages for heavy smokers, because there are no more drastic reductions.

From now on, the target is to get down to the Addiction Threshold and no further. You are going to cut down, but gradually; at no point will you suffer, but neither will you indulge yourself.

On day one you are going to smoke twenty. On day two it will be nineteen, on day three eighteen, and so on. Each day you take a pack of twenty and remove those you are not going to smoke. You put them away so that in effect they no longer exist for you.

On the sixth day you will take out five cigarettes from a new pack and put them with your collection. This means that on day seven you need fourteen cigarettes but you will already have fifteen saved up, so you don't need to open a new pack. This is the first day of the programme when won't have opened a pack of cigarettes.

Three days later you need eleven cigarettes and you have sixteen in your collection already, so again you don't need to open a new pack. The following day you need ten but you have five already, so a fresh pack will last you two days. A this point a pack of twenty is lasting two days or more. You've achieved a lot. It's time to take a break.

Stage 4
It's a good idea to spend the next week as a ten-a-day smoker. But this doesn't mean you can relax – it means you concentrate on not smoking more than ten. In this phase you are vulnerable. Your motivation might weaken; you might see life as a non-smoker looming before you and it might look frightening. But remember that you are still in control. You are still a smoker. No one is telling you to stop except you: this is all entirely voluntary. You could go back to smoking twenty, thirty, forty or whatever. If you do, that's not the end of the world. You have come this far, and you can come this far again. It would just be a great shame not to see if, having come this far, you really can win.

Read through once more the chapters of the book that are most important, particularly Chapters 8 and 10.

Stage 5
This is the final stage of the Preparation Programme. You are now going to reduce your smoking from ten a day to the Addiction Threshold. This might be four, five or six a day, but you will know you have hit it because you will start to feel some withdrawal symptoms – don't go this far. Once you have hit your target, stay there. How long you stay there is up to you. Some people will want to stay there for a while and get really comfortable with being a very light smoker. Others will want to move straight on. Whichever you do is fine. You will have planned the Cessation Programme long before this point, so it is ready when you are.

Before you move on, spare a thought for your success. You have reduced your smoking by a tremendous amount. Perhaps you used to believe this wasn't possible, but you have just proved that it is. The hardest part of stopping smoking is not the habit, stress or anything else. All of the psychological issues are within your control, as long as:

* You want to exercise that control.
* You have read the book and understood the issues.

The rest of this chapter contains an at-a-glance week-by-week schedule, plus a more detailed account of roughly where you should be in each week of the programme. You will probably have variations – just use these charts for quick reference.

Schedule

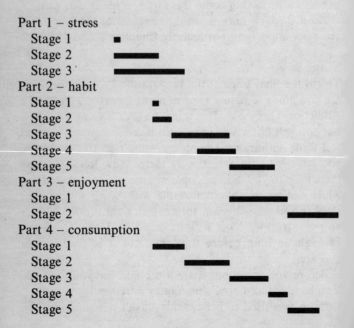

Week 1 2 3 4 5 6 7 8 9 10 11 12 13 14 15

Part 1 – stress
   Stage 1
   Stage 2
   Stage 3
Part 2 – habit
   Stage 1
   Stage 2
   Stage 3
   Stage 4
   Stage 5
Part 3 – enjoyment
   Stage 1
   Stage 2
Part 4 – consumption
   Stage 1
   Stage 2
   Stage 3
   Stage 4
   Stage 5

Week-by-week guide

Week 1   Complete your stress barrel.
Start learning your breathing exercises.
Sign up for relaxation or yoga classes.

Week 2   Keep working on your breathing.
Have you started your relaxation classes?

Week 3   Your breathing should be improving by now.
You are practising your relaxation or yoga.
You should start to feel less stressed.

Week 4   Work out your habit target cigarettes.
Stop smoking your first target cigarette.
Keep working on the breathing and relaxation.
If you smoke sixty a day, reduce to forty now.

Week 5   Stop smoking your second target cigarette.
Stay off your first target cigarette as well.
Concentrate on your breathing and relaxation
exercises.

Week 6   Eliminate your third target cigarette (cup of tea
or coffee).
Stay off your other target cigarettes.
Don't stop the breathing and relaxation exercises.

Week 7   Eliminate smoking with tea and coffee
altogether.
Stay off your other target cigarettes.
Your breathing and relaxation exercises
are even more important now.
If you smoke forty a day, reduce to twenty now.

Week 8   Go back to smoking your first target cigarette.
Stay off all your other target cigarettes.
Keep working on your breathing and relaxation
exercises.

Week 9   Continue to stabilize, as week 8.
Your breathing should be more natural by now.
You should be feeling fairly relaxed about it all.

Week 10 Eliminate any other habit cigarettes you want to.

Eliminate your first enjoyment target cigarette.

Start reducing from twenty a day.

You should be enjoying your relaxation/yoga exercises.

Week 11 Keep getting used to doing without your first enjoyment target cigarette.

Keep the consumption going down at a steady pace.

Stay relaxed, breathe well all the time.

Week 12 Same as week 11 to stabilize.

Take relaxation seriously – you're going to need it.

Week 13 Your lucky week – you reach the Addiction Threshold.

Stop cutting your consumption.

Eliminate your second enjoyment target cigarette.

Keep relaxing.

Week 14 Stabilize at your Addiction Threshold.

Stabilize without two enjoyment target cigarettes.

Stop worrying about the next stage – relax.

Week 15 The world has not collapsed. Keep doing it.

In fifteen weeks, look at what you have achieved:

* You are a very light smoker.
* You have little fear of stopping.
* You are in control of your stress response.
* You can change your habits at will.
* You are looking forward to making further progress.
* You are ready to stop smoking.

15

The Cessation Programme

Before you start, make sure you have read Chapter 10 so that you don't expect too much too soon. At this point you should have completed the Preparation Programme, but if you still don't feel ready please don't proceed. It would only be a half-hearted attempt, and another failure could finish off your resolve to ever try again. Just go back to the Preparation Programme and persevere with it a little longer until you feel more confident.

Part 1 – dipping your toe in the water

Just keep remembering that instant success is not what we are after. It has a nasty way of leading to instant failure.

In Part 1, you are going to experience being a non-smoker while you are still a smoker, if that doesn't sound too confusing. What you will actually be doing is trying out being a non-smoker without challenging your addiction too much, and without challenging your psychological dependence at all; this is because you will still be a smoker for a while, and that security will stop the fear.

At all times remember that what the future holds does not concern you. You are concerned with the next twenty-four hours only. Now you have a choice. From the following list select a time during the week to practise being a non-smoker:

* A whole day, during the week.
* A whole day, at the weekend.
* Half a day, during the week.
* Half a day, at the weekend.
* Waking up, and the first two hours.

It doesn't matter which you take, so choose the one you think you will cope with best.

Why are we asking you to subject yourself to what seems like torture? First, it isn't torture really. Most smokers, regardless how many they smoke, can sit through a film or a long meeting without a cigarette. For light smokers (twenty-a-day or fewer) the worst withdrawal symptoms will start on the second day. Second, it *is* torture if you think you are never going to smoke again: the fear of the future magnifies the withdrawal terribly. But you *can* smoke again, so you are learning to handle the withdrawal symptoms (which are inevitable) without the fear.

Third, it is a kind of game. At the moment smoking still controls you, even though you have cut down considerably, but you are learning that you can control smoking. Finally, even though you will suffer from withdrawal symptoms, this rehearsal is well worth it for the valuable experience. When you finally go through it for real it will not seem so terrible, because you will have a memory of overcoming it.

So decide when your smoke-free time is going to be, and do it. Don't feel you have to do any more at this stage, although there is no harm in doing so. If you do want to do more, make it at least a day away from your first smoke-free time.

Assuming you are sticking to just one smoke-free time at this stage, make a note of your symptoms, thoughts and feelings during it. As each smoke-free time comes round, record your symptoms again and compare them week by week. When you are feeling more confident, it is time to move on. This is unlikely to take less than four weeks, but don't be tempted to let it drag on either.

Part 2 – taking the plunge

When you are stabilized on one or two smoke-free times each week, and you are used to low-level withdrawal symptoms, you are ready to move on. You will probably also be feeling impatient at this stage, which is how it should be. This is the point you have been working for all this time. Now you will understand why we have been taking you through this whole process so slowly, and apparently back to front. Every other stop-smoking method tells you to stop smoking and then sort out the mess. But with our method your mess should be well and truly sorted out by now. If you have any doubts at all, delay taking the plunge for a few days while you read through the book again.

Before proceeding, answer these questions:

* Are you smoking at the Addiction Threshold?
* Do you have at least one smoke-free time each week?
* Are you still doing your breathing and relaxation work?
  Have you made serious changes to your smoking habits?
  Are you more confident than when you started the programme?

If the answer to all these questions is Yes, then pass GO and collect £200 (two months' cigarette money? How much have you saved so far?).

Timing

Putting off the fateful day is something that most smokers do. But you, on the contrary, may well be raring to go. You are already more than halfway to being a non-smoker, so there is no point in stopping the programme now.

171

Here are some last-minute things to do before you stop smoking:

* Get a supply of *vitamin C tablets*, and start taking 3000mg a day immediately. Keep taking them until we tell you to stop. They are going to speed up the detoxification process which you will undoubtedly go through. And drink as much *water* as you can manage.
* It is sometimes recommended that you stop drinking *tea and coffee* at this point, or at least change to decaffeinated, because the caffeine will be more potent when you stop smoking. The effect can be similar to withdrawal symptoms. It is not necessarily a good idea to stop altogether, because you might easily be addicted to caffeine, and we never recommend patients to come off more than one addiction at a time. But you should certainly cut down on the coffee, particularly if you drink, say, more than five cups a day.
* *Make certain decisions*. Are you going to tell everyone you are stopping, so they can support you? Or are you going to keep it a secret, so they can't pressure you? Are you going to throw your cigarettes and lighter and ashtrays away, so you aren't tempted? Or are you just going to hide them so you still have your security blanket? (But see also the next point on this list.)
* Throw away (or hide, depending on what you decided to do) *all your cigarettes except one*. You will see why shortly.
* Cancel all boozy *social engagements* for the next week at least.
* Get in a supply of *low-sugar but filling foods*. You need food that will fill you up and satisfy your oral desire without making you put on a lot of weight, such as wholemeal bread, potatoes and pasta. It's important not to hit the sugar over the next few weeks, because you

blood-sugar regulation will be upset when you stop smoking and a lot of sugar in your body will make the withdrawal harder.
* Book *a day off from work* or domestic duties for the second day of the Cessation Programme.

Day one

On the day you stop smoking, you are going to take the one cigarette you have saved and smoke half of it. When that half is gone, stub the rest out, throw it away and wash out the ashtray.

Why do we ask you to smoke half a cigarette? Wouldn't it be better just to stop the night before and start afresh?

No. The time of your strongest craving, as you know well, is early morning. That is not a good way to start the day and your career as a non-smoker, because you need to smoke before you even start. By smoking half a cigarette you will get a small fix of nicotine which will get you going. Don't forget, you have already been without the drug for perhaps eight hours overnight, so do yourself a favour and just relieve the craving a little.

If you don't smoke at all that morning, you have got a whole day to get through from a starting point of craving. But by doing it our way, by the time you go to bed the craving will not be much worse than it normally is first thing in the morning, and sleep will help greatly. By the time you wake up the next morning you will already have done your first twenty-four hours as a non-smoker, and you won't have died or gone berserk and killed anyone.

Day two

If in the morning of the second day you can get up and get out (at possibly the most critical time for your addiction, remember), you will get through this time without too much pain. Don't hang around the house waiting for something to go wrong. This day won't be like any other. Trying to pretend it is not happening, by continuing with your normal routine, is asking for trouble. Day two needs to look as different as possible, so indulge yourself and make it a holiday. If you work, take a day off as mentioned above, and take yourself off somewhere. To coin a phrase, it is the first day of the rest of your life.

By now you will be feeling the withdrawal from nicotine. If you are considering smoking to cope with the symptoms, ask yourself a question. Is the withdrawal so terrible that I am prepared to smoke for the rest of my life rather than suffer for a few days?

It is vital for you to recognize that the symptoms cannot go on for more than a few days. What you have to weigh up is these days of suffering against a one-in-four chance of death. At no time are withdrawal symptoms worse than lung cancer, emphysema or the loss of your legs.

It is also vital that you spend two minutes, at least four times a day, doing your breathing and relaxation exercises. Now you know why they are so important: learning them properly could be the difference between smoking and not smoking at this time.

Remember that the easiest thing in the world would be to smoke, in which case you will never again know what it feels like to be a non-smoker. Accept this challenge. You have no choice but to go through with it if you want the freedom to choose – to be a smoker or a non-smoker.

When you get home from your day out, prepare yourself an indulgent meal, but don't have a glass of wine with it if that would be a trigger to smoke. If you would normally watch television after dinner, read a book instead. Go to bed early with a good book (or your partner – remember, indulge yourself). Now you have completed another day.

Day three

You have now been a non-smoker for two days, and you are about halfway through the withdrawal from your drug. If you can go through just another couple of days you will come out of the withdrawal phase. Remember, every day you have not smoked you are getting further away from the addiction. Just think yourself lucky it takes only four days and not four weeks!

Day four

By now the withdrawal symptoms might be subsiding. If they are not, the chances are that your fear is making them worse. It is just not possible for withdrawal to last more than a few days, so after today you are into a new phase, one in which you will be challenging your psychological dependence – the addiction's last line of defence.

Day five

If you are still desperate to smoke, you should be able to observe a definite change in your symptoms. The need to smoke is now more emotional than physical. Any physical symptoms have subsided, to be replaced by psychological ones. The most common symptom we note in our patients at this stage is panic. As long as you are having withdrawal symptoms, you are still addicted, which is comforting (even if subconsciously) if you are in conflict about stopping, which you will be.

Because you are no longer addicted to nicotine, you now have to face the future without cigarettes. No longer is it possible to bluff yourself that you might fail, because you are succeeding. Go back through those chapters of the book which you think will be most helpful at this stage. But don't try to do this on your own – use the book for support, and feel free to call the NHA Helpline for advice. And continue to work hard at your relaxation exercises.

You have now completed the Cessation Programme. If you are still smoking at this point, you are not yet ready to move on. So go back to the beginning of the Cessation Programme, or even back to the Preparation Programme. But whatever you do, don't stop working, because you have come too far for that. There's no turning back now.

16

The Maintenance Programme

Conventional stop-smoking advice says you stop smoking first, then deal with the chaos it causes – the really hard part. There are, as you will know by now, two distinct periods of difficulty:

* Nicotine withdrawal, which takes a few days.
* Psychological dependence, which can last forever.

So the conventional advice would appear to be back to front. But by working through the Preparation Programme before the Cessation Programme, you should now find yourself a non-smoker who is rather battered from the last few days, but intact none the less.

Part 1 – the short term

You are no longer addicted

One of the biggest mistakes people make at this stage is to believe they are still addicted. But if you have understood this book you will know that, if you haven't smoked for four or five days, you are no longer addicted. You could (but won't) prove this: if you smoked a cigarette now, it would taste awful. This means that you have lost your adaptation to nicotine, and adaptation equals addiction. If you can't stand the taste, it's impossible to be addicted still. Be absolutely clear on that.

What you are, as you also know by now, is psychologically dependent. If you are addicted, you cannot control the symptoms of withdrawal. But when you are psychologically dependent you can, and must, control those symptoms. You have been brainwashed by the drug into believing you must always have it, and it is that brainwashing that is standing between you and freedom.

In a totalitarian dictatorship, the people genuinely believe in the benevolence of their leader. This is not really surprising: it is always easier to abdicate responsibility for your life. But you owe it to yourself not to submit to the dictatorship of tobacco. Breaking free is full of doubts and fears, but *being* free is wonderful.

What you must do now

Accept that your motivation will waver. You are coming off the most insidious drug you can buy; this will challenge your determination. Either you will win, or the drug will.

Stay away from smokers. They will often try to get you smoking again, because they know they should stop but can't, so the next best thing is for you to fail. If a smoker persists in offering you a cigarette after you have said you don't smoke, just take it and crush it in your hand. He or she will get the message.

Stand up for your rights. Many new ex-smokers allow people to smoke in their home because they don't want to dictate to them. You have the right to decide that smoking is banned in your home. No one has a right to come into your home and take a drug that kills three hundred people a day, and once threatened to kill you. Not even if they live there!

Keep busy. Many people at this stage expect just to get on with their lives as if nothing had happened. Something *has* happened – you have stopped using a drug that was shortening your life. Get out and about, enjoy yourself in new ways, indulge yourself, treat yourself. And be gentle on yourself, because you are convalescing, and this take time. You are also grieving for the loss of your drug. You have been bereaved, so give yourself time to come through this.

Stop feeling guilty. It's common to feel you are a fool for getting yourself into this mess. You are not a fool, and you didn't get yourself into any mess.

Relax. Now is the time to be practising your breathing exercises several times a day, as well as the other relaxation exercises you have learnt. If you are in control of your stress response, no problem is going to make you smoke again.

Keep your sugar consumption down. There are two reasons. First, you might be comfort eating for which sugar is good – but it is also exactly the thing that is going to make you overweight. So find something else for comfort eating.

The second reason is that smokers regulate their blood sugar with nicotine (you have probably experienced the appetite suppression you can get from smoking). When you stop smoking this facility is no longer available and your body instinctively seeks sugar instead. So if you don't keep your sugar consumption down now you will get into a cycle of sugar/insulin highs and lows, known as hypoglycaemia. This effect is often misinterpreted as withdrawal.

The mistake of your life

Many smokers make a tragic mistake at this point. They weigh up the problems they are now having and decide they would be better off smoking. Don't do it. Not only will smoking shorten your life, but there is also another factor of which you must constantly remind yourself.

Non-smokers don't have the problems you are having. You are having them not because you don't smoke but because you used to smoke. If you start smoking again, you will have exactly the same problems if you try to stop again. So what you are in effect deciding, if you give in to the problems now, is that you are going to smoke for the rest of your life. Many people give in to this and regret it for the rest of their lives. There is no problem you are experiencing that can be worth taking a drug that is going to shorten your life.

Assume that if you are not lucky enough to die of a heart attack you will get lung cancer, emphysema, or have one or both legs amputated. Even if this is only a twenty-five per cent chance, it has to be taken seriously. Are your present problems worth this chance? It might take you three months to overcome these problems, but how long does it take to get used to a wheelchair? How long does it take to get used to having to use an oxygen cylinder all day? How long does it take to get used to having one lung?

Remember, it is not necessarily death that you are facing. That would not be so difficult. It is years of crippling disease and dependence on others – still abusing yourself with the drug that crippled you in the first place. You are likely to be denied treatment by the NHS because you suffer from what they term a self-inflicted disease. And you will be forced to spend perhaps £1,000 a year (at today's prices) on the drug that caused your illness, with a dwindling income as you get older and more diseased.

You can give in to the drug, or you can be free.

Tobacco fights back

We have discovered a key stage in our clinical programmes. It happens two to four weeks after stopping (bear in mind that our patients are having their addiction stopped medically, so their timing might differ from yours).

At this point you might well find your previous success and optimism suddenly replaced by doubt and increased cravings. Don't worry – this is quite normal. There is a perfectly logical explanation.

When you start to stop, you really don't know if you are

180

going to succeed. A small part of your subconscious is hoping that you will fail, whether you admit it or not. Of course it does, because you are addicted. After two or three weeks of not smoking, that success is looking awfully real. This triggers your subconscious to accept the horrible possibility that you really won't ever smoke again. Suddenly the future is the present, and it is a future you had not really learnt to accept – because it might never happen.

At this point your motivation collapses. You interpret the effect as withdrawal symptoms – but remember you cannot possibly be having these because you are no longer addicted. Your psychological dependence is able to mimic all the normal withdrawal symptoms and make you very vulnerable. If you can use your conscious desire to be a non-smoker to overcome your subconscious desire to fail, you will win.

Part 2 – the medium term

Statistics tell us that three-quarters of ex-smokers go back to tobacco within three months. This suggests that your initial target is three months, because that will presumably get you out of the danger zone. If this is true, everything you have learnt in this book so far will get you to that point.

After three months as a non-smoker, what challenges do you still face?

Challenge: given that you never wanted to stop in the first place – not 100 per cent – you will now be wondering why you bothered, particularly if you have felt no immediate health benefit. This is because you are definitely still psychologically dependent. If you smoked for, say, thirty years, three months is not a long time by comparison.

Solution: remind yourself *why* you wanted to stop. Those reasons haven't changed. You were simply expecting your life to change in an unreasonably short time.

Challenge: you still miss smoking. You had hoped you could forget you had ever smoked.

Solution: remember that every cigarette you have ever smoked is in your memory, and always will be. It isn't possible to forget you were once a smoker. Once you can accept this, it will be easier to live with the memory. Time is the greatest healer.

Challenge: you still get a strong desire to smoke when you see other people enjoying a cigarette.

Solution: start to think like a non-smoker. You don't smoke. Non-smokers can watch people 'enjoying' a cigarette and see them as no more than drug addicts. Try it (but don't tell them – you wouldn't have liked it when you smoked). You can smoke whenever you want to; the only person who stopped you is you. So you must have had a very good reason.

Some counsellors in smoking cessation tell people that they are going to be ex-smokers, not non-smokers. But this is negative and defeatist. Ex-smokers get offered cigarettes by smokers. They are constantly reminded about smoking. How can this attitude conceivably help? So take the following words to heart.

You are not an ex-smoker. You are a non-smoker. Whether you once smoked is now irrelevant.

Part 3 – long term

There are four reasons why long-term ex-smokers (we use the expression here for a good reason) go back to smoking.

First, they will always remember what they thought was the 'enjoyment'. This challenges their motivation forever, and makes them vulnerable. To deal with this one reread Chapter 8. Make sure you really accept that the 'enjoyment' was part of the addiction.

Second, they remember that smoking helped them when

they were stressed. Coming under severe stress will make them smoke again. To deal with this there are two solutions. Reread Chapter 9 to remind yourself that smoking causes more stress than it relieves. And never stop practising your breathing exercises. You owe it to yourself to stay as stress-free as possible. You cannot know what stressors will hit you in life, so protect yourself by altering your stress response permanently. Good diaphragmatic breathing is your best defence.

Third, they forget to not smoke. At a party or in a similar social situation it is easy, after a few drinks, just to accept a cigarette without thinking, smoke a couple, buy a pack to return the favour, smoke ten that evening, and wake up the next morning addicted. It's a bit like getting pregnant after a one-night stand – it was fun at the time but you'll pay for it forever. The solution is to think like a non-smoker, not like an ex-smoker. A non-smoker would not accept a cigarette. A nun would not get pregnant.

Fourth, ex-smokers will, from time to time, be tempted to think they could go back to being a 'social smoker', or just smoking for the occasional pleasure, without getting addicted again. But it is possible to be a 'social smoker' if, and only if, you have never been addicted. Once you have been addicted your adaptation mechanism will recognize nicotine again straightaway, and you will become readdicted faster than you can light a match. In this sense you are an ex-smoker, rather than a non-smoker, for life. But don't worry about it – as long as you don't smoke, you won't become readdicted.

Part Three

Further Help and Information

17

The A.N.T. Story

When we found the Addiction Neutralisation Therapy
(A.N.T.) which was being used in just one NHS hospital
in the 1970s we were excited, but we did not realize the
enormity of what we were taking on. Little did we know
how desperately the treatment was needed, or how difficult
it was going to make our lives.

When the NHA was launched in the late 1980s, it was
almost certain to confuse the medical establishment. Never
before had there been anything like it. It was to be non-
profit, but run professionally. It would not register as a
charity because this would restrict its political activities, and
we knew that healthcare provision is partly controlled by
politics. It was to work exclusively with conventionally
qualified doctors, nurses, nutritionists and other practitioners, and yet it would have no truck with the pharmaceutical companies, because these companies wield
immense power over the provision of medical treatment
in the UK. It would make every effort to foster good
relations with the National Health Service, and particularly GPs working within the NHS, but it would not bow to
pressure to conform to established practices if these were
not serving the public well.

In short, it was to achieve the impossible. Much to
everyone's surprise, the impossible became possible, and
then it actually happened.

The function of the NHA is to develop what we call
'socially sustainable medicine'. This means a move away

from very high-technology medicine, which may make vast profits for drug companies but actually reduces the control that individuals have over their own healthcare. We know that, in many areas of medicine, relatively simple techniques exist which are not being promoted only because there is no profit in them for anyone. Medical research funding in the UK is dominated, both directly and indirectly, by the drug companies.

One area in which the NHA is working is Crohn's disease (see page 23). There is a simple and inexpensive treatment which is achieving up to eighty per cent success against this disease, and this has been verified within the NHS at Addenbrooke's Hospital in Cambridge. This is one of the projects that receive funding from NHA Stop-Smoking Clinics.

We have three strict criteria before taking on a new project:

* Is the therapy needed but not available within the NHS?
* Is the therapy a medical one? In other words, does it justify the special expertise of the doctors in the NHA?
* Is the therapy absolutely safe?

We had these three conditions in our minds when we looked at the work done by Dr Richard Mackarness at Basingstoke District Hospital. Dr Mackarness was a specialist in environmental medicine, and he brought some important techniques from the USA where he did much of his training. The work he was doing at Basingstoke involved neutralizing the reaction suffered by people who are seriously allergic to certain foods or other environmental triggers. This work, which has been taken up by a dedicated group of doctors in Britain, has benefited tens of thousands of people. Without it, this book could not have been written: partly because it led to the development of the techniques we use in NHA clinics, and partly because without the treatment I would not have been alive to write it.

What Dr Mackarness did that was so extraordinary was to reason that what would work for allergy would work for addiction. It surprises patients to learn that there is a connection, and even some doctors are unfamiliar with it. This is how it works, in very simple terms.

You are familiar with the concept of an 'acquired taste', but have you ever considered how you acquire a taste? Almost everyone who smokes disliked the taste of their first cigarette, and you are unlikely to be an exception. This is no different from foods – for example tea and coffee, alcoholic drinks and a lot of the ordinary things you eat on a daily basis but did not like as a small child.

When you think about it, there is no reason why you should like the taste of something completely new to you, is there? The reason you acquire the taste is because there is pressure on you to do so; with foods, your parents encouraged you to develop adult tastes, but with cigarettes the pressure probably came from your friends. You smoked the first one because of that pressure, and even though you hated it, you persisted until you acquired the taste.

If you get to like something, you are naturally going to want it again. This is already a kind of dependence, because your body is saying, 'I didn't like it at first but you forced me to like it and now I do. If you don't give it to me I shall lose the taste, which probably means you are going to force me to acquire the taste all over again, which I would prefer not to do. So give it to me, now.'

When a patient is allergic to something, their immune system thinks that the substance in question is a poison and it reacts by producing the symptoms of being poisoned. Because the substance is not a poison at all, the symptoms are inappropriate and the patient is unwell. We don't know yet why some people react in this way, but it is interesting to note the use of the word 'poison' here. Tobacco, by any standards, is clearly a poison. There is enough nicotine in one cigarette alone to kill the average adult if injected into the bloodstream.

Allergy and addiction

Many people are allergic and have no idea that they are, because they suffer no symptoms. How does this square with what we have just been saying about the immune system producing unwanted symptoms? This is what we call masked allergy. The body becomes dependent on a substance and produces no symptoms for as long as it gets a regular dose (typically once every four days).

This is proved in allergy clinics by eliminating the suspect substance from the patient's diet for at least four days. The food is then reintroduced in controlled conditions, when the patient may have a violent reaction to the food. This comes as quite a shock, because they have been eating that food for years. This shows how the body adapts to poisons, or what it thinks are poisons.

As we said, tobacco too is a poison. That the body adapts to it at all is quite amazing. The reason it does so, and so quickly, is that nicotine is a narcotic drug. The brain likes it even if the body hates it, and the brain wins because it is a powerful drug. So the brain has adapted within days. The body takes rather longer to adapt to the delivery method – poisonous burning gases.

Your current smoking can be thought of as a masked allergy. As long as you keep doing it, your body has the ability to handle the assault we call smoking. Stop doing it, even for one day, and your body desperately tries to hold on to its adaptation. After all, it is quite logical that, if the body fights for its adaptation to a minor poison such as alcohol it is going to fight harder to remain adapted to a major one.

Anyone can be allergic; in fact it is true to say that the entire population is potentially allergic in that they could demonstrate allergy symptoms. So everyone has the mechanism we call adaptation built into them, controlled by their immune system.

So when you learn to smoke, you are forcing your immune system to create a mechanism for dealing with the poison. The downside is that that mechanism does not allow for withdrawal of the poison – you have to keep supplying it to your body to remain adapted. This state is addiction.

Addiction neutralization

What Dr Mackarness was doing for allergy sufferers at Basingstoke District General Hospital is called neutralization. This process introduces a minute amount of the allergen (the substance to which the patient is allergic) into the body. There is enough for the immune system to recognize the substance and create a resistance to it, but not enough to produce symptoms. It is rather like the standard immunization procedure for diseases such as polio and whooping cough.

If it is possible to 'persuade' the immune system not to react to an allergen (remember, this is a substance which the body mistakes for a poison), Dr Mackarness wondered, could the immune system also be persuaded not to react to real poisons? He tested his patients for their Endpoint (called the Addiction Level in this book), which is their individual reaction to an allergen and indicates what proportion of the allergen can be used to provide immunity, but in this case the allergen was tobacco.

He then gave the patients the correct dose of the substance, and found that the immune system deactivated itself. In other words, it stopped asking for the substance it needed to maintain its 'acquired taste', or dependence.

In the field of addiction, he had found the holy grail. Because this was an entirely new medical intervention, no medical term existed for it. The substance used is like a vaccine, but the NHA has coined the word 'neutrogen' to describe it. Both terms are used in this book, as is Addiction Neutralization Therapy or A.N.T.

Dr Mackarness put hundreds of patients through the treatment, and all of them reported relief from withdrawal symptoms. Without the support of an integrated smoking cessation programme, though, these patients achieved no very exciting rate of success for stopping smoking. This clearly demonstrates that there is no single reason for not being able to stop smoking.

We looked at the results of Dr Mackarness' work, and wondered what we could do to capitalize on his extraordinary success. We asked the obvious question: 'If the technique is so good, why isn't every doctor in the country using it?'

The answer was simple. The technique is not enough on its own, and Dr Mackarness himself could go no further because he was not a specialist in stop-smoking methods. But Dr Mackarness, now in Melbourne, was delighted that his work was going to be developed by others in the UK. We then looked for a doctor who had been trained in the techniques in allergy work brought from the USA by Dr Mackarness.

We started a monthly clinic for smokers, in Hove, Sussex, charging only a nominal fee because we could not guarantee success. We built into the programme our ideas on psychological dependence and stress management, and we gave people an all-important telephone helpline, partly so that we could help them, but also partly so we could learn from their reactions.

We subsequently opened clinics in Eastbourne and London as well, and what we learned from these first few hundred patients was the three reasons for the failure of so many smoking cessation methods.

Solving Smokers' Problems

First, we learned that there are many reasons for not being able to stop, that they are the same for most smokers, but that they vary in relative importance between smokers. This meant that no one method was going to help all smokers. What we needed was to find the best in every known therapy and combine these into one super-programme. This book is, in fact, about what we have learnt from our thousands of patients.

Second, we learned that, although everyone in the stop-smoking field was busy telling patients not to worry about addiction, it is of crucial importance. Without it, there would be no psychological dependence.

Third, we learned that controlling addiction was not enough on its own, and conventional psychology was not enough on its own, but that the two combined – all the best smoking cessation psychology, without nicotine withdrawal symptoms, works. Just how well it works has surprised everyone who has seen the results of our clinical work, which you will find expressed in non-technical terms on pages 196–8.

Before we even got as far as the aims and protocols of the clinics, we laid down three very important criteria, and these criteria apply now to all our clinical work.

1. No patient under the age of thirty will be accepted

This is because, whether we are conducting research or providing treatment to fee-paying patients, we restrict the treatment to those who are likely to take it seriously. We

193

consistently find younger smokers lacking in motivation, and more interested in miracle cures. Although it was difficult to maintain this criterion with some of the trials, we are stricter in our private clinics.

2. No patient smoking fewer than twenty cigarettes a day will be accepted

Although it can be just as difficult to stop smoking ten a day as sixty a day, patients have quite a high commitment when entering an A.N.T. programme, and we find heavy smokers are more motivated. They also have more to gain. Interestingly, we tend to find that heavier smokers are better patients. Of course, as the aim of A.N.T. is to stop smoking completely on the day of the treatment, going from sixty a day to zero in two hours can seem rather dramatic.

3. No smoker who cannot demonstrate a history of failed attempts will be accepted

This is partly because we need to see that the smoker has real motivation. It is also because, as a non-profit research company, we are very careful not to compete with commercial companies. Almost all our private patients have previously been on nicotine patches. That they are still smoking does not mean that patches are ineffective; it simply means that our patients used them and are still smoking. Because A.N.T. is the opposite of the patch – it is not a tobacco substitute – smokers who have used substitutes understandably believe they need something completely different, and the concept of a neutrogen interests them.

We do not, however, insist on these strict criteria in every case. How could we turn down a twenty-five-year-old asthmatic, or a sixty-five-year-old with a heart condition (who cannot therefore use patches), or a pregnant woman who only smokes fifteen a day?

The clinics

When you run demonstrations you need to be very clear what exactly you are setting out to prove. Smoking is not like any of the diseases normally targeted in clinical trials, because there is no single cause.

Everyone told us that the obvious question to ask was, 'Does A.N.T. stop people smoking?' We already knew the answer to that question. No, it doesn't. Nothing stops people smoking. People stop themselves smoking. In other words, people have control over whether they smoke or not. And they therefore have control over the success of any stop-smoking therapy. It is vital in a conventional drug trial that the trial subjects have no control over their treatment. They need to be treated, as far as possible, just like animals in a laboratory.

So it is quite impossible, in a trial of stop-smoking therapy, to ask such a simple question and get a simple answer. However, all stop-smoking therapies are measured by this simplistic criterion, which is why the results of trials are so meaningless. It is far more relevant to ask some rather more complex and sophisticated questions:

* Why don't people want to stop smoking? (Because if smokers were totally motivated to stop, they would succeed.)
* Why can't people stop smoking? (How much is attributable to the different reasons – addiction, habit, psychological dependence, stress, social pressure?)
* What do current stop-smoking methods achieve? (Do they tackle single issues, like habit, with substitutes?)
* What happens if you combine single-discipline therapies? (Like substitutes for habit, counselling for motivation, and stress management techniques?)
* How much does addiction matter? (It is always said

that, since it is over in a few days, it isn't important. If it isn't important, why can't people stop smoking? You just go round in circles with that argument.)

We felt the eyes of the stop-smoking world were upon us when we started the clinics. That we refused to accept their conventional criteria left us wide open to criticism. But 111,000 smokers are dying every year, no one has a claim to complete authority in this field.

We asked ourselves the obvious question. If so many people fail attempts to stop smoking, and even more won't make an attempt through fear of failure, and even more don't want to stop because they don't believe they can, what is missing from current stop-smoking methods?

We found only one answer. Most smoking 'cures' deny the importance of addiction. And since we had developed a highly powerful addiction treatment, what else could we do but see if it made the difference?

As you will see from our results, it did.

1994 results
Demonstration clinics for GPs
Neutrogen efficacy

Question: How effective is the neutrogen (vaccine)? Level of craving at the end of a day with neutrogen instead of tobacco:

Clinic 1
Pharmaceutical company, London, fifteen patients, all employees

Little or no craving	15	100 per cent
Quite a lot	0	
A lot	0	
Too much	0	

Clinic 2

Kent County Council, eleven patients, all probation officers.

Little or no craving	11	100 per cent
Quite a lot	0	
A lot	0	
Too much	0	

Clinic 3

South Bedfordshire Community Health Care Trust, twenty patients, all members of the public

Little or no craving	18	90 per cent
Quite a lot	2	10 per cent (one subsequently stopped)
A lot	0	
Too much	0	

Clinic 4

Aston University, Birmingham, thirty-five patients, all members of the public

Little or no craving	32	91 per cent
Quite a lot	3	9 per cent (still in the programme)
A lot	0	
Too much	0	

Clinic 5

Claremont Hospital, Sheffield, twenty-six patients, all members of the public

Little or no craving	24	92 per cent
Quite a lot	2	8 per cent (still in the programme)
A lot	0	
Too much	0	
Total patients	107	

Number showing little or no craving
  on neutrogen   100
As a percentage   93 per cent

Notes:
1. Those who still had quite a lot of craving were not ready
to stop smoking immediately and were put on gentler
programmes. The typical reduction in smoking with this
type of patient is 80–90 per cent for the first few weeks,
before they are ready to stop.
2. The NHA does not publish long-term results. We are
hoping for funding for this from the Department of Health.
3. There has been no recorded incidence of adverse reaction
to the neutrogen, from a total of 3,546 patients.

18

You Need Friends

If someone you care about is trying to stop smoking, or is just thinking about trying, please read this. It will help you to understand what they will be going through and how you can help them.

If you feel like reading the whole book, by all means do so. You might be surprised, and the more you know the more helpful you can be.

You gave up, so why can't they?

You might be an ex-smoker yourself, in which case your views on stopping will be dominated by your own experience. But please don't assume what happened with you is the same for everyone. Have an open mind about the great variety of reactions that can occur, without condemning the person you are supposed to be helping.

Why do they want to stop anyway?

You might even be a smoker who doesn't want to stop. There are a number of reasons why people don't want to stop, and if you are interested this book explains them. What we are not going to do is try to convince you that you *should* want to stop – that's up to you. We do find it difficult in our clinics when a patient lives with someone who doesn't want to stop. What they sometimes say is that their partner is quite happy for them to come to us, and they will try the programme 'if it works'. If you say this to your partner (whatever method they are using) you are actually putting them under pressure, partly because they feel they are being scrutinized, and partly because they probably want you to stop, and feel they have to prove to you it can be done.

A true friend will support unconditionally someone who is trying to stop.

You've never smoked and it's time they pulled themselves together

If you've never smoked, you are likely to be puzzled about all the fuss being made about stopping. You may not realize that:

* Almost every smoker is addicted to nicotine, a narcotic drug as addictive as heroin. Don't confuse addiction with habit; addiction is a chemical response in the brain over which the smoker has no control whatever.
* A long-term smoker is usually psychologically dependent. This means that, no matter how much they want to stop, they simultaneously have a very deep fear of succeeding.
* Addiction and psychological dependence are not the same at all. Addiction is the brain's chemical response, dependence is in the mind. Addiction cannot be controlled by the mind, it is simply suffered; dependence is under the control of the smoker, but it takes a lot of work, and time, to overcome it.

To say that a smoker is afraid of succeeding probably seems strange to you. They say they want to stop, so why would they be afraid of succeeding? To understand this fully you would need to read the whole of this book, but here is a brief explanation.

Just imagine you had been married for forty years and

your husband or wife suddenly died. One of your immediate emotions would be the thought of spending the rest of your life without them. Even in couples who had been thinking of divorcing, a bereavement can be very painful.

For someone trying to stop smoking, the thought of being without their prop for the rest of their life is often frightening, however much they want to be free of smoking. This is the same as a bereavement – even if someone wants to be free of their partner, or when the partner has been ill for a long time, the end of the relationship still comes as a shock, and the thought of being without their companion is frightening.

If you have been divorced, you might know this feeling. Whilst planning to separate, you wanted to get on with it, but there was perhaps also some trepidation because you were stepping into the unknown.

Similarly, ex-smokers need a lot of time to grieve over their loss, even though they imposed it on themselves. This is a time of great temptation. In a marital separation it is not uncommon for one of the parties at least to toy with the idea of getting back together. This clinging to what is known and safe is a natural process that simply has to be gone through.

A new non-smoker going through this process is vulnerable. Cigarettes are readily available. To return, even briefly, to what is known and safe is a comforting idea, even if it goes against all the wishes and dreams of being a non-smoker.

So if you are going to help someone you care about through this time, try to see them as someone who has been through a bereavement. It is tempting when they are trying to stop smoking to say, 'Come on, pull yourself together. They were disgusting and you're better off without them.' This might seem appropriate support, but would you talk like this to someone whose partner had died?

Give them a chance to discuss their feelings, while being

supportive. They have suffered a self-imposed bereavement. Telling them the cigarettes were their enemy might seem helpful but it often isn't, because they are missing their prop, and they are in conflict. A more understanding approach is called for; something like, 'Yes, you've done it now, and I know it's painful but you can come through.'

Your hostility to their smoking is not going to help. They might even have stopped *because* of you, so give them credit for what they are going through.

This need for something they have been trying to divorce themselves from is what we mean by psychological dependence.

So what practical help can you give, besides being supportive? Everyone who stops smoking goes through much the same process but each person's reaction to the process is different, and each smoker is the best judge of what is best for themselves, depending on their own circumstances.

If you are a smoker yourself

We find most smokers are supportive to those trying to stop. The exception tends to be those who have a psychological need for those around them to continue smoking, because this justifies and reinforces their own position as a smoker. It is not uncommon for a smoker, particularly in the workplace, to goad another into starting again.

If you are trying to stop smoking, this can make someone who is not look foolish for not trying. Every smoker knows that what they do is 'wrong', but they justify it in various ways. When someone close to them stops, they can feel foolish for continuing. This can lead them to encourage the other person to start again.

It is hard to believe that anyone could be that selfish, particularly if they are a friend or partner, but it really does happen.

If you smoke, and someone close to you wants to stop, give some thought to your response. If you don't support their efforts, ask yourself if you might feel this way out of jealousy, and whether you could help them without feeling that it in any way condemns your own desire to continue smoking.

If you are an ex-smoker

However you stopped smoking, you are likely to believe that your way is the best way to do it, or even the only way. When we were gathering support for our own research into nicotine addiction we had some correspondence with a well-known TV presenter who had stopped smoking. Her attitude was that any smoker who wanted to stop should just grit their teeth and stop making a fuss, and that they should not mess about with asking anyone for help because you have to do it on your own. She might have done this herself, which would explain why she tried to justify her bizarre attitude; but meanwhile, every day that smokers are not getting the help they need another three hundred die.

Every manufacturer of cures for smokers, every fringe practitioner, every book on stopping (except this one of course!) says theirs is the only true answer. They all offer some 'divine truth' which is going to change the smoker's life.

Everyone who helps people stop smoking does so ultimately for profit. This applies to individual practitioners, purveyors of remedies, writers and health authorities. Health authorities, like everyone else, are paid for what they do, and a small part of what they get paid for is helping people stop smoking.

Anyone who profits is in the business of selling something. And anyone who is selling something wants people to buy their product, service or idea rather than any other. But in this context smoking is not like an illness that can be cured, and it is not amenable to any single product or service.

When you stopped smoking, however you did it is going to be 'the' way to do it. If your partner has tried the same method, and failed, you are going to conclude that there is something wrong with your partner.

Your partner has a problem which is individual to him or her. If every smoker is exactly the same, and they all know smoking is going to cause their premature death, why are fourteen million people still doing it when you managed to stop? If you did it, why can't everyone? Perhaps everyone doesn't want to stop, but then of course they do if three hundred people die each day. This line of reasoning is going to get you nowhere. You simply have to accept that, however you overcame smoking, it might not be appropriate for your partner.

So if your partner is reading this book, and figuring out how finally to overcome their smoking problem, please support them in whatever they decide to do.

This book is not promising them a miracle cure. It is a programme for them to follow in calm, logical steps. It is first going to help them to understand what they need to do, then it is going to lead them through the steps. These steps will not always be forwards, and here is something we would like you to keep in mind at all times. There is more than one way to succeed. Success does not have to be instant, and in the case of someone with a history of failure it is unlikely to be. Each step forward must be supported and congratulated. Each step backward must be understood. The most important rule is this – *never* tell your partner they have failed if they smoke one cigarette; in fact as long as they are smoking less than they used to, they are making progress. What are you going to do – stop them trying?

It is possible that, when you stopped smoking, you just threw away what cigarettes you had left. This is not appropriate for everyone. Some people prefer to do this, because it removes the temptation. Some need to have a pack around the house, or hidden in the car, like a security blanket. Someone who is heavily dependent on a drug can benefit tremendously from knowing that they *could* have it if they needed it. With our patients, knowing that the cigarettes are there if needed is often enough to reduce the level of stress that is inevitable when they stop. Ironically, a would-be ex-smoker can be more likely to give in to temptation and go and buy some, because the possession of the cigarettes can be as important as smoking itself. And having just bought them, they are far more likely to smoke them than if they were already lying in the spare room or the glove compartment.

If you have never smoked

A non-smoker is likely to think someone that trying to stop is making an unnecessary fuss. Having read this far, you should now understand this is not so. Even if you cannot put yourself in the same position as your partner (and they are likely to remind you of this – they will always say to non-smokers, 'You've never done it so you can't imagine what it's like', and they are right), if you care about them you will simply accept that their problems are genuine.

Your partner is working their way through the programme in this book. It all makes sense to them, if not to you.

Some rules for all friends and relatives

* Don't blame them for having been a smoker.
* Don't put them under pressure.

* Don't offer them a cigarette when they come under stress.
* Don't be accusing if they need just the occasional cigarette.
* Do let them follow the programme their own way.
* Do let them set their own timetable.
* Do understand if they keep a pack of cigarettes in the house.
* Do congratulate them every day they make progress.

19

Smoking and Asthma

Cigarette smoking has two opposing effects on the bronchi (air tubes) of the lungs. On the one hand, the complex mixture of tars and combustion products includes many allergens (substances which allergy-prone individuals are likely to react to), and therefore certain people tend to become allergic to cigarette smoke. Since allergy in the lungs leads to asthma, smoking tends to make allergic smokers worse.

On the other hand, the smoke also contains nicotine and other drug-like constituents which relax the bronchi and loosen the mucus so it can be coughed up. Many asthmatics find that a deep draw on a cigarette helps them cough up their phlegm and breathe more easily. Fifty years ago doctors used to recommend smoking for asthmatics for this reason.

Thus smoking is doing two things at once, one good and one bad, for asthmatics. The 'good' action – relieving the breathing – is fast and easily noticed. The 'bad' effect – aggravating the allergy – is slow and not easily recognized by the sufferer; it takes many years to cause a gradual and insidious deterioration of lung function.

Asthmatics who stop smoking may find their asthma aggravated. Smokers who never had asthma may develop it – for the first time in their lives – after quitting. This is because they no longer enjoy the short-term relief afforded by the smoke. We therefore consider it essential that allergy to smoke (when it exists) is treated at the same time as quitting.

In practice this is easily brought about by the neutralization technique described in this book. As well as abolishing or reducing the addiction, it abolishes or reduces the allergy. In our experience so far, patients who are effectively neutralized for tobacco smoke do not develop asthma when they quit, and those who were already asthmatic get better, not worse. As with non-allergic ex-smokers, the patient's need for the neutrogen diminishes with time, although asthmatics are likely to need the drops for somewhat longer, especially when subjected to passive smoking.

20

Help and Support

At the NHA we spend our lives giving people the best help and the best advice we can. We hope this book has been helpful to you; that, even if you don't stop smoking now, you will give careful thought to what we have said and find the right time to change your life. You have nothing to lose by trying. If you would like to talk to us about it, please don't hesitate to call the NHA Helpline.

Remember the most important truth you will ever need to know while you stop smoking:

> You are faced with problems because you want to stop smoking. If you had never smoked, these problems would not exist, so it is smoking that has caused your problems. Smoking is not, and never has been, a friend to you.

And remember the most important truth you will need to know after you have succeeded:

> Because you once smoked tobacco, and were a nicotine addict, you will remember your smoking days with pleasure, always, no matter how happy you are now to be a non-smoker. There might be times when you would prefer to be back there, because you only remember the good times. If you allow that to happen, tobacco will finally have won.

The NHA National Helpline

This Helpline is not a premium cost line; you will pay only the normal telephone cost. It is also not a recorded message.

Our function at the NHA is to talk to smokers, so your call will be answered by a qualified smoking cessation counsellor, who will be interested to hear about your progress through *Stop Smoking for Good* and will help you with any problems or questions.

The number to call is 01273 424185 and it is usually manned Monday–Friday, 9am–6pm.

If you have difficulty getting through, please remember that we are an non-profit company, and we do the best we can with the limited resources we have.

Thank you for reading this book, and good luck.